ANIMAL ATLAS

CLAIRE LLEWELLYN

SCHOLASTIC INC.

New York Toronto London Auckland Sydney
Mexico City New Delhi Hong Kong

Text: Claire Llewellyn
Consultant: Sandi Bain, Education Officer, London Zoo
Main illustrations: Steve Roberts (Wildlife Art Agency)
Computer illustrations: Mel Pickering, Jacqueline Land
Managing editor: Deborah Kespert
Editor: Samantha Hilton
Editorial support: Flavia Bertolini, Inga Phipps, Amanda Nathan
Art director: Belinda Webster
Senior designer: Helen Holmes
Picture research: Laura Cartwright
U. S. editor: Melissa Tucker, World Book Publishing

ISBN 0-439-13044-1

12 11 10 9 8 7 6 5 4 3 2 1   9/9 0 1 2 3 4/0

Printed in the U.S.A.   08

First Scholastic printing, September 1999

Photographic credits: BBC Natural History Unit/Pete Oxford p9, BBC Natural History Unit/Rico & Ruiz p25 b, BBC Natural History Unit: p40 tl; Britstock-IFA/AP&F Fernandez & Peck p33, Britstock-IFA: p40 tr; Bruce Coleman Ltd/John Shaw p8, Bruce Coleman Ltd/Jorg & Petra Wegner p10 b, Bruce Coleman Ltd/Marie Read p13 t, Bruce Coleman Ltd/Joe McDonald p13 b, Bruce Coleman Ltd/Erwin & Peggy Bauer p17 t, Bruce Coleman Ltd/Gordon Langsbury p23 b, Bruce Coleman Ltd/Hans Reinhard p24, Bruce Coleman Ltd/Dieter & Mary Plage p37 t, Bruce Coleman Ltd: p38 b, p39; NHPA/Manfred Danegger p22, NHPA/Gerard Lacz p32 b, NHPA: p38 t; Oxford Scientific Films/Wendy Shattil & Bob Rozinski p10 t, Oxford Scientific Films/John Mitchell p12, Oxford Scientific Films/Richard Day p16 b, Oxford Scientific Films/Bob Bennett p27 t, Oxford Scientific Films/Mickey Gibson p28, Oxford Scientific Films/Andrew Plumptre p32 t, Oxford Scientific Films/Frank Schneidermeyer p37 b, Oxford Scientific Films: p42; Planet Earth Pictures/Carol Farneti p16 t & p18 t, Planet Earth Pictures/David A. Ponton p23 t, Planet Earth Pictures/Ken King p25 t, Planet Earth Pictures/Pete Oxford p26, Planet Earth Pictures/Ronald Rogoff p30 t, Planet Earth Pictures/Nick Greaves p30 b, Planet Earth Pictures/M&C Denis p31; The Stock Market: p19, p36, p43; Telegraph Colour Library/Steve Bloom cover; Tony Stone/David E. Myers p11, Tony Stone/Norbet Wu p18 b, Tony Stone/Art Wolfe p27 b, Tony Stone/Manoj Shah p29.

Contents

How to use this book — 4

World map — 6

The Arctic and Antarctica — 8

Canada — 10

The United States — 12

Florida Everglades — 14

Mexico, Central America, and the Caribbean — 16

South America — 18

Galapagos Islands — 20

Northern Europe — 22

Southern Europe — 24

Russia and its neighbors — 26

Southwest Asia — 28

Northern Africa — 30

Southern Africa — 32

Madagascar — 34

Southern Asia — 36

Eastern Asia — 38

Southeast Asia — 40

Australia, New Zealand, and the Pacific Islands — 42

Great Barrier Reef — 44

Glossary — 46

Index — 47

How to use this book

The maps in this book show you where lots of different animals live, from polar bears in the freezing Arctic to scorpions in the scorching desert. Look below to find out how to use the maps. You'll also find a helpful glossary and index at the back of the book.

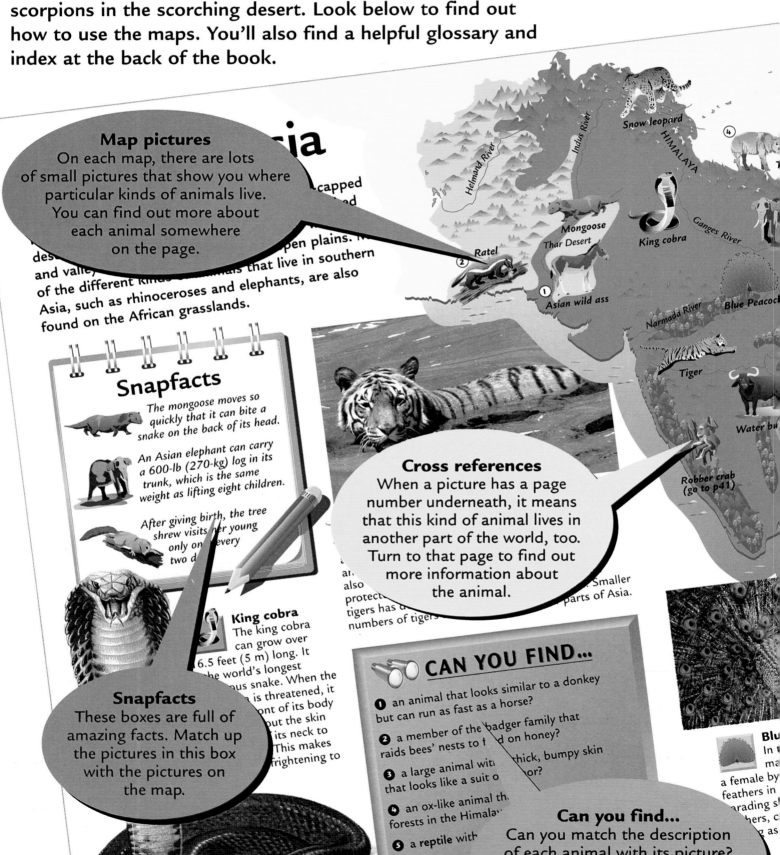

Map pictures
On each map, there are lots of small pictures that show you where particular kinds of animals live. You can find out more about each animal somewhere on the page.

Snapfacts
The mongoose moves so quickly that it can bite a snake on the back of its head.

An Asian elephant can carry a 600-lb (270-kg) log in its trunk, which is the same weight as lifting eight children.

After giving birth, the tree shrew visits her young only on[ce] every two d[ays]

King cobra
The king cobra can grow over 6.5 feet (5 m) long. It [is t]he world's longest [venomo]us snake. When the [snake] is threatened, it [lifts fr]ont of its body [and p]uts the skin [around] its neck to [...] This makes [...] frightening to

Snapfacts
These boxes are full of amazing facts. Match up the pictures in this box with the pictures on the map.

Cross references
When a picture has a page number underneath, it means that this kind of animal lives in another part of the world, too. Turn to that page to find out more information about the animal.

CAN YOU FIND...
❶ an animal that looks similar to a donkey but can run as fast as a horse?
❷ a member of the badger family that raids bees' nests to f[ee]d on honey?
❸ a large animal wit[h] thick, bumpy skin that looks like a suit o[f armo]r?
❹ an ox-like animal th[at ...] forests in the Himala[ya?]
❺ a reptile with [...]

Can you find...
Can you match the description of each animal with its picture? Each clue is numbered and matches up with a numbered picture on the map.

Asia

[...]capped [...] [...] pen plains. [...] [...] that live in southern Asia, such as rhinoceroses and elephants, are also found on the African grasslands.

Helmand River
Indus River
Snow leopard
HIMALAYA
④
Mongoose
Thar Desert
King cobra
Ganges River
Ratel
②
①
Asian wild ass
Narmada River
Blue Peacoc[k]
Tiger
Robber crab (go to p41)
Water bu[ffalo]
Smaller parts of Asia.

Blu[e ...]
In t[...] ma[...] a female by [...] feathers [...] [p]arading [...] [...]hers, c[...] [...]g as

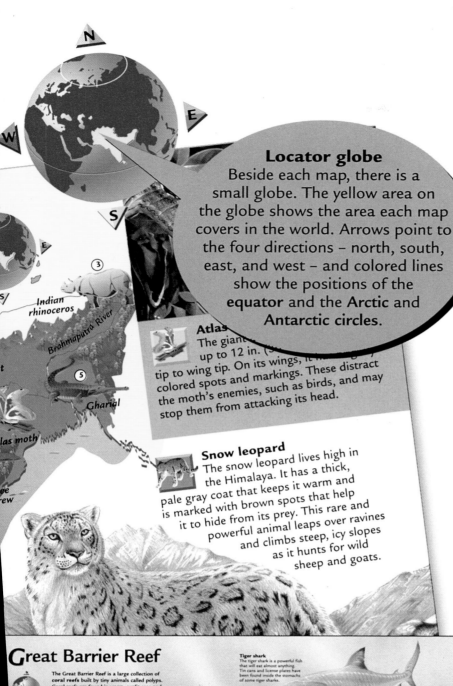

Locator globe
Beside each map, there is a small globe. The yellow area on the globe shows the area each map covers in the world. Arrows point to the four directions – north, south, east, and west – and colored lines show the positions of the **equator** and the **Arctic** and **Antarctic** circles.

Indian rhinoceros

Brahmaputra River

Gharial

Atlas moth

Atlas
The giant ... up to 12 in. (... tip to wing tip. On its wings, it has ... colored spots and markings. These distract the moth's enemies, such as birds, and may stop them from attacking its head.

Snow leopard
The snow leopard lives high in the Himalaya. It has a thick, pale gray coat that keeps it warm and is marked with brown spots that help it to hide from its prey. This rare and powerful animal leaps over ravines and climbs steep, icy slopes as it hunts for wild sheep and goats.

Great Barrier Reef

The Great Barrier Reef is a large collection of coral reefs built by tiny animals called polyps. Coral reefs are found in warm, sunlit seas and are teeming with a rich variety of wildlife, from graceful sea anemones and groups of brightly colored fish, to prickly starfish and fierce sharks.

Tiger shark
The tiger shark is a powerful fish that will eat almost anything. Tin cans and license plates have been found inside the stomachs of some tiger sharks.

Cowfish
The cowfish's square-shaped body is made of such rigid, bony plates that the fish can move only its mouth and fins.

Crown-of-thorns starfish
The crown-of-thorns starfish turns its stomach inside out onto the coral and eats it.

Sea anemone
The sea anemone is an animal that looks like a plant. It anchors itself to the coral and waves its long tentacles through the water.

Anemone fish
The anemone fish has a slimy covering on its body that protects it from the sea anemone's stinging tentacles.

Giant clam

45

37

Special places
There are eight pages that explore special areas of the world. These are unique habitats that are home to a variety of animals, some of which are found nowhere else.

Animal habitats
The place where an animal lives is called its habitat. Below, you can see the different types of habitats that are shown on the maps in this book.

Rivers are large streams of water. Some swell to form lakes. Others travel down to the sea.

The land around the poles, in the far north and south of the world, is extremely cold and icy.

Grasslands are flat, dry areas covered by grasses and scattered with a few trees.

Evergreen forests stay green all year. They grow on mountains and in cold northern parts of the world.

Deciduous forests grow in cool parts of the world. The trees lose their leaves in winter.

Deserts are dry places, where there is little rain. They can be hot or cold, rocky, or sandy.

Tropical rain forests are thick green forests that grow in hot, wet places near the equator.

Mountains are high rocky hills where the weather is windy and cold.

World map

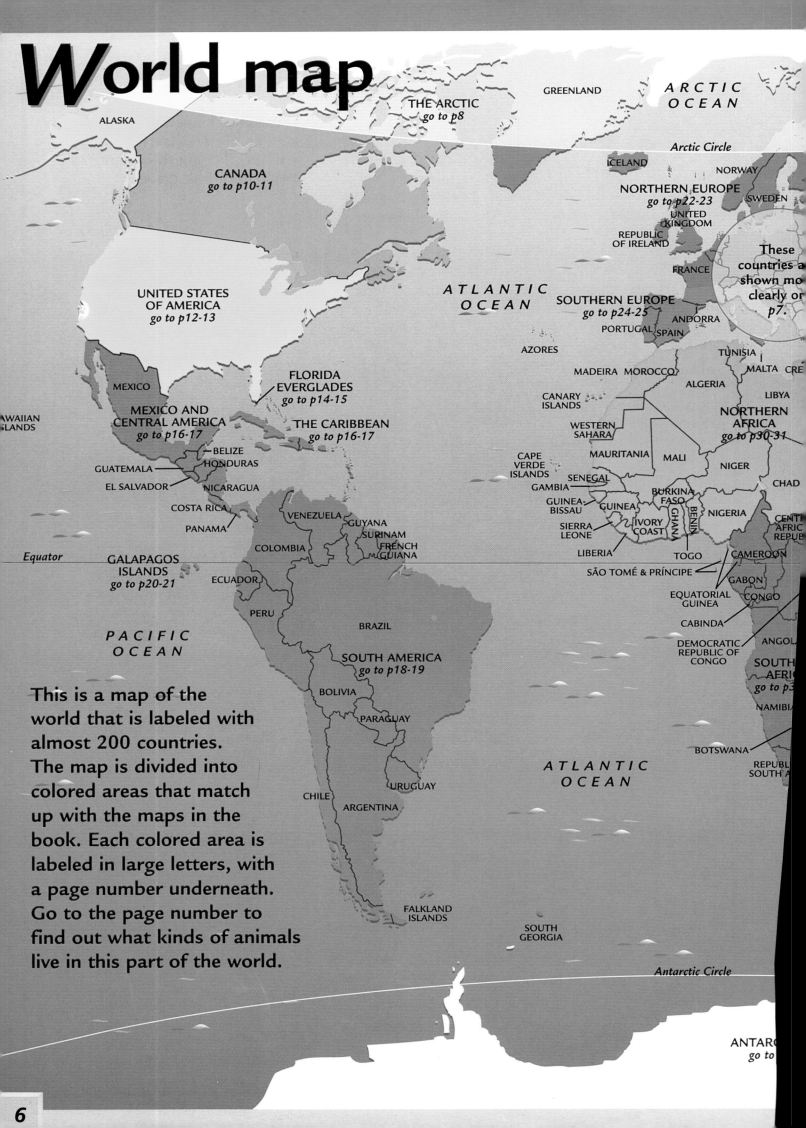

GREENLAND

THE ARCTIC
go to p8

ARCTIC
OCEAN

ALASKA

Arctic Circle

ICELAND

NORWAY

CANADA
go to p10-11

NORTHERN EUROPE
go to p22-23

SWEDEN

UNITED
KINGDOM

REPUBLIC
OF IRELAND

FRANCE

These
countries a
shown mo
clearly or
p7.

UNITED STATES
OF AMERICA
go to p12-13

ATLANTIC
OCEAN

SOUTHERN EUROPE
go to p24-25

ANDORRA

PORTUGAL SPAIN

AZORES

TUNISIA

MADEIRA MOROCCO

MALTA CRE

ALGERIA

LIBYA

MEXICO

FLORIDA
EVERGLADES
go to p14-15

CANARY
ISLANDS

NORTHERN
AFRICA
go to p30-31

MEXICO AND
CENTRAL AMERICA
go to p16-17

WESTERN
SAHARA

AWAIIAN
SLANDS

THE CARIBBEAN
go to p16-17

MAURITANIA

MALI

NIGER

BELIZE

CAPE
VERDE
ISLANDS

SENEGAL

HONDURAS

GUATEMALA

BURKINA
FASO

CHAD

GAMBIA

EL SALVADOR

NICARAGUA

GUINEA-
BISSAU

GUINEA

NIGERIA

COSTA RICA

VENEZUELA

GUYANA

SIERRA
LEONE

IVORY
COAST

GHANA

BENIN

CENTF
AFRIC
REPUB

PANAMA

SURINAM

COLOMBIA

FRENCH
GUIANA

LIBERIA

TOGO

CAMEROON

Equator

GALAPAGOS
ISLANDS
go to p20-21

ECUADOR

SÃO TOMÉ & PRÍNCIPE

GABON

EQUATORIAL
GUINEA

CONGO

PERU

CABINDA

BRAZIL

PACIFIC
OCEAN

DEMOCRATIC
REPUBLIC OF
CONGO

ANGOL

SOUTH AMERICA
go to p18-19

SOUTH
AFRIC
go to p3

This is a map of the
world that is labeled with
almost 200 countries.
The map is divided into
colored areas that match
up with the maps in the
book. Each colored area is
labeled in large letters, with
a page number underneath.
Go to the page number to
find out what kinds of animals
live in this part of the world.

BOLIVIA

NAMIBI

PARAGUAY

BOTSWANA

REPUBL
SOUTH A

ATLANTIC
OCEAN

URUGUAY

CHILE

ARGENTINA

FALKLAND
ISLANDS

SOUTH
GEORGIA

Antarctic Circle

ANTARO
go to

THE ARCTIC
go to p8

LAND

TONIA

ATVIA

RUSSIA AND ITS NEIGHBORS
go to p26-27

KRAINE

AZERBAIJAN

KAZAKHSTAN

MONGOLIA

ARMENIA

GEORGIA

UZBEKISTAN

KYRGYZSTAN

NORTH
KOREA

JAPAN

TURKEY

RUS

TURKMENISTAN

TAJIKISTAN

EASTERN ASIA
go to p38-39

SOUTH
KOREA

SYRIA

LEBANON

AFGHANISTAN

CHINA

PACIFIC
OCEAN

JORDAN

IRAN

IRAQ

KUWAIT

BHUTAN

AEL

BAHRAIN

PAKISTAN

NEPAL

MACAU

TAIWAN

PT

SAUDI
ARABIA

QATAR

UNITED
ARAB
EMIRATES

INDIA

SOUTHERN ASIA
go to p36-37

MYANMAR

HONG
KONG

NORTHERN
MARIANAS

SOUTHWEST ASIA
go to p28-29

OMAN

BANGLADESH

LAOS

VIETNAM

GUAM

DAN

ERITREA

YEMEN

SOCOTRA

ANDAMAN
ISLANDS

THAILAND

CAMBODIA

SOUTHEAST ASIA
go to p40-41

MARSHALL
ISLANDS

DJIBOUTI

PHILIPPINES

PALAU

ETHIOPIA

NICOBAR
ISLANDS

BRUNEI

MALDIVE
ISLANDS

SRI
LANKA

STATES OF MICRONESIA

UGANDA

SOMALIA

MALAYSIA

KENYA

SINGAPORE

INDIAN
OCEAN

NAURU

KIRIBAT

RWANDA

BURUNDI

INDONESIA

IRIAN JAYA

TUVALU

TANZANIA

SEYCHELLES

PAPUA NEW
GUINEA

AMBIA

COMOROS

MALAWI

MAYOTTE

SWEDEN

LATVIA

LITHUANIA

SOLOMON
ISLANDS

THE PACIFIC
ISLANDS
go to p42-43

MADAGASCAR
go to p34-35

DENMARK

(Russia)

BELARUS

GREAT
BARRIER
REEF
go to p44-45

VANUATU

BABWE

THE NETHERLANDS

POLAND

FIJ

MOZAMBIQUE

GERMANY

UKRAINE

AUSTRALIA

NEW
CALEDONIA

BELGIUM

LUXEMBOURG

CZECH
REPUBLIC

SWAZILAND

LIECHTENSTEIN

SLOVAKIA

FRANCE

AUSTRIA

HUNGARY

MOLDOVA

OTHO

SWITZERLAND

SLOVENIA

ROMANIA

AUSTRALIA AND
NEW ZEALAND
go to p42-43

MONACO

SAN
MARINO

CROATIA

FEDERAL
REPUBLIC OF
YUGOSLAVIA

BOSNIA AND
HERZEGOVINA

TASMANIA

ITALY

BULGARIA

CORSICA

TURKEY

SARDINIA

MACEDONIA

NEW ZEALAND

VATICAN
CITY

ALBANIA

GREECE

SICILY

Some countries in Europe are
close together. In this circle, we
have made these countries bigger so
that you can see them more easily.

7

The Arctic

The Arctic is an icy area in the far north of the world. Summers here are short and chilly. Winters are long and dark, with snowstorms and freezing winds. All the animals that live in the Arctic have a thick layer of fat, fur, or feathers to keep out the bitter cold.

Arctic fox

During the winter, the arctic fox's coat changes from brown or gray to pure white. This helps the fox to hide in the snow. Arctic foxes are quick-footed animals that eat almost anything, including **birds'** eggs, **fish,** and hares.

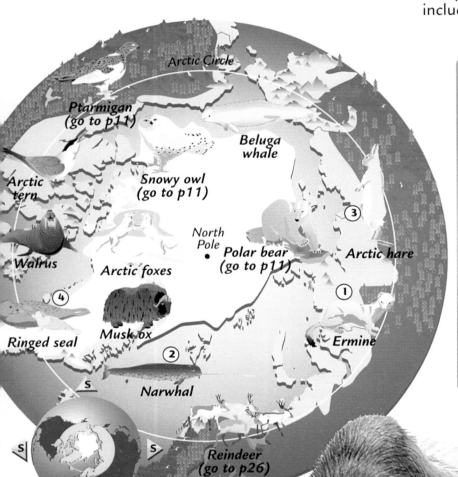

Arctic Circle

Ptarmigan (go to p11)

Beluga whale

Arctic tern

Snowy owl (go to p11)

North Pole

Polar bear (go to p11)

③

Arctic hare

Walrus

Arctic foxes

④

①

Musk ox

Ermine

Ringed seal

②

Narwhal

Reindeer (go to p26)

Snapfacts

Arctic terns fly from the Arctic to Antarctica and back. That's a round trip of over 21,000 miles (36,000 km)!

A walrus's ivory tusks can grow as long as baseball bats.

Beluga whales used to be called sea canaries because they talk to each other with noisy clicks and chirps.

Musk ox

The musk ox has an extremely thick coat of dark, shaggy fur. It lives in herds on the **tundra,** which is a bleak, treeless plain on the edge of the Arctic. When a pack of wolves threatens the oxen's young, the herd stands in a ring around the young and the oxen lower their heads. They make a solid wall of sharp horns that the wolves dare not attack.

CAN YOU FIND...

❶ a member of the weasel family whose fur was used in the past to make coats and capes?

❷ a small whale with a long, spiraling tusk on its head?

❸ a hare with short ears that keep it from losing too much heat?

❹ a seal with ringlike markings on its fur?

Antarctica

Antarctica is a giant, ice-covered **continent.** It is the windiest place on Earth. Few animals live on the frozen mainland, but the warmer surrounding ocean is full of **fish** and creatures such as whales, squid, and krill. In summer, seals and **birds** come to **breed** on the rugged coastline.

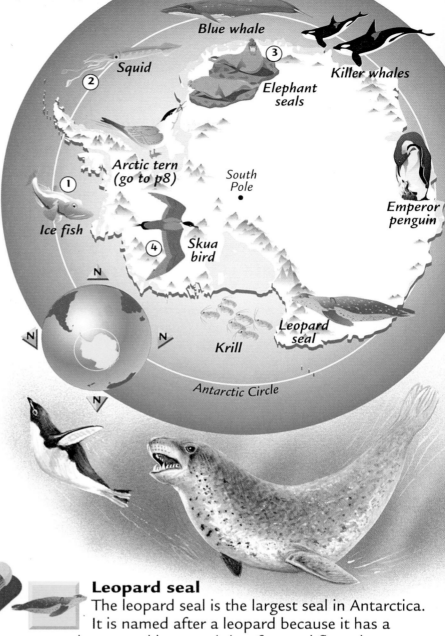

Blue whale

Squid

②

③

Killer whales

Elephant seals

Arctic tern (go to p8)

South Pole

①

Ice fish

Emperor penguin

④

Skua bird

N

N

N

N

Krill

Leopard seal

Antarctic Circle

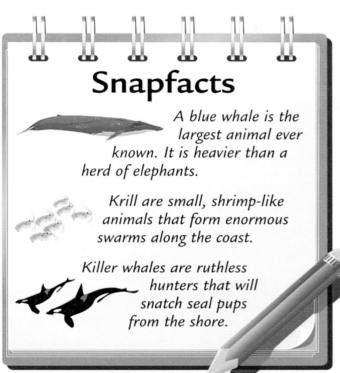

Snapfacts

A blue whale is the largest animal ever known. It is heavier than a herd of elephants.

Krill are small, shrimp-like animals that form enormous swarms along the coast.

Killer whales are ruthless hunters that will snatch seal pups from the shore.

Leopard seal
The leopard seal is the largest seal in Antarctica. It is named after a leopard because it has a spotted coat, and because it is a fast and fierce hunter. It chases squid, fish, and penguins through the water, catching them with its powerful jaws and sharp teeth.

Emperor penguin
The emperor penguin is surprisingly tall, standing about as high as a person's waist. A female lays just one egg, which the male keeps warm on top of his feet until the penguin chick hatches. These birds survive the bitter winter by huddling together in huge groups called rookeries.

CAN YOU FIND...

❶ a fish that has special blood in its body that prevents it from freezing in icy water?

❷ a soft-bodied animal that squirts out a dark ink when it is threatened?

❸ a member of the seal family that bellows through its large, swollen nose?

❹ a bird with a hooked beak that steals other birds' eggs?

Canada

Canada is a huge country with rugged mountains; dense, evergreen forests; long, winding rivers; and crystal-clear lakes. These places provide homes for many different kinds of animals. Winters are bitterly cold, especially in the far north. Some types of animals have **adapted** to the cold, and others **migrate** south to warmer areas.

Arctic Circle

Mackenzie River

Yukon River

Great Bear Lake

Wolverine (go to p23)

Grizzly bear

Great Slave Lake

Ptarmiga

Wolf (go to p27)

Mink

ROCKY MOUNTAINS

Bobcat

Raccoon

Snowy o

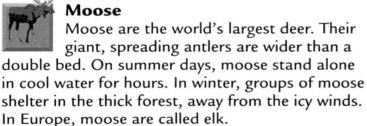

Moose
Moose are the world's largest deer. Their giant, spreading antlers are wider than a double bed. On summer days, moose stand alone in cool water for hours. In winter, groups of moose shelter in the thick forest, away from the icy winds. In Europe, moose are called elk.

Grizzly bear
Grizzly bears are huge, strong animals that live in remote mountain forests. In summer, groups of grizzlies gather at the edges of fast-moving rivers to snatch up **fish** with their gigantic paws. In winter, grizzly bears find shelter under rocks or fallen trees and sleep peacefully until spring.

Raccoon
With its two eye patches, the raccoon's face looks like a mask. During the day, it sleeps in a hollow log or tree. At night, the raccoon climbs through the trees, gripping the branches with its long fingers. It steals eggs and chicks from nesting **birds** for its food.

Polar bear

The polar bear is the world's biggest bear. A male can weigh more than five people. Polar bears have thick fur coats and layers of fat beneath their skin that keep them warm. When they hunt seals, which are their main **prey**, their white fur **camouflages** them against the snow. A female usually gives birth to twin cubs, which stay with their mother until they are about 2 years old.

Ermine
(go to p8)

Polar bear

Hudson Bay

son
River

Moose

Beaver

Skunk

St. Lawrence River

Monarch butterfly

Great Lakes

Cod

3

Harp seal

1

CAN YOU FIND...

1 a sea animal that is caught in huge numbers by fishermen for food?

2 a bird of prey whose legs are covered in warm, white feathers?

3 a sea creature that lives in groups of up to one million off Canada's eastern coast?

4 an animal with a bushy tail that is hunted for its thick fur?

5 a wild cat whose coat helps it to hide in the forest?

Snapfacts

The beaver's two front teeth never stop growing. If they did, gnawing through tree trunks would wear them down!

*In winter, the ptarmigan's brown feathers turn white to **camouflage** the bird in the snow.*

The skunk drives its enemies away by showering them with a stinking spray from behind its tail.

Monarch butterfly

The monarch butterfly is an expert flier. It spends summer in Canada, but in winter, groups of monarchs travel more than 1,800 miles (3,000 km) to the southern United States and Mexico. The butterflies spend the winter resting in the sunshine before their return journey in spring.

The United States

The United States has a hugely varied landscape and **climate**. Eagles soar over the snow-covered Rocky Mountains, and in the southern deserts, lizards and snakes shelter from the hot sun. Herds of grazing animals once roamed vast, empty grasslands in the center of the country. Most of this land is now used for farming.

ALASKA

Arctic Circle

Bald eagle

Salmon

Chipmunk
The chipmunk feeds on nuts and seeds, which it nibbles with its two sharp front teeth. It stores the food in pouches inside its cheeks and then carries it back to its underground burrow. The chipmunk's burrow has several snug chambers, or rooms, where it lives, nests, and sleeps.

Bald eagle
This white-headed eagle is the national symbol of the United States. It earned its name long ago when the word "bald" meant "white." A bald eagle lives far from cities. It is a sharp-eyed hunter that dives into rivers and lakes to catch **fish** in its curved talons.

Snapfacts

The bison, commonly known as the buffalo, is the heaviest animal native to the U.S. It can weigh more than 15 people.

Salmon return to the stream where they were born to lay their eggs. On the way, they swim upstream and leap over high waterfalls.

The pronghorn can run almost 50 miles (80 km) per hour.

Prairie dogs
These strong, short-legged animals are members of the squirrel family. They live underground and dig large networks of tunnels, called prairie towns. More than 500 prairie dogs may live together in one town. They "talk" to each other by barking and touching teeth.

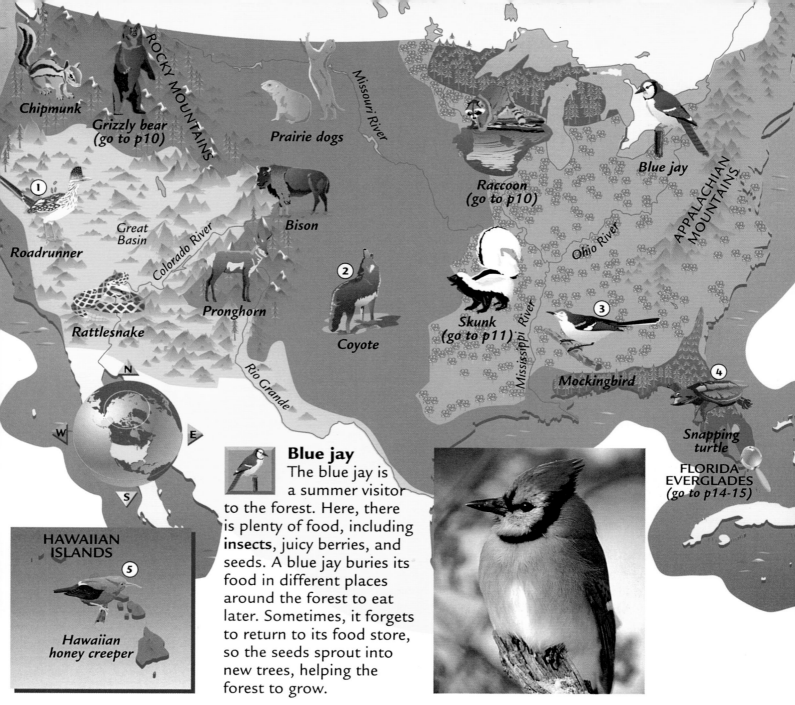

Chipmunk

ROCKY MOUNTAINS

Grizzly bear
(go to p10)

Prairie dogs

Missouri River

Raccoon
(go to p10)

Blue jay

APPALACHIAN MOUNTAINS

① Roadrunner

Great Basin

Colorado River

Bison

Ohio River

Skunk
(go to p11)

② Coyote

Pronghorn

Mississippi River

③ Mockingbird

Rattlesnake

Rio Grande

N

W   E

S

④ Snapping turtle

FLORIDA EVERGLADES
(go to p14-15)

HAWAIIAN ISLANDS

⑤ Hawaiian honey creeper

Blue jay
The blue jay is a summer visitor to the forest. Here, there is plenty of food, including **insects**, juicy berries, and seeds. A blue jay buries its food in different places around the forest to eat later. Sometimes, it forgets to return to its food store, so the seeds sprout into new trees, helping the forest to grow.

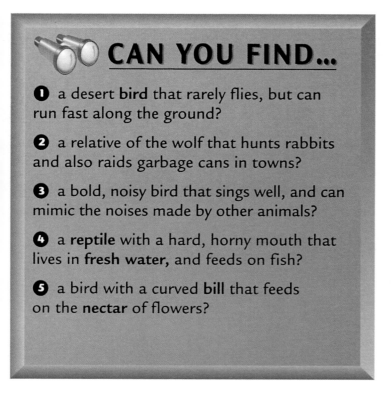

CAN YOU FIND...

❶ a desert **bird** that rarely flies, but can run fast along the ground?

❷ a relative of the wolf that hunts rabbits and also raids garbage cans in towns?

❸ a bold, noisy bird that sings well, and can mimic the noises made by other animals?

❹ a **reptile** with a hard, horny mouth that lives in **fresh water,** and feeds on fish?

❺ a bird with a curved **bill** that feeds on the **nectar** of flowers?

Rattlesnake
The rattlesnake attacks by biting animals and pumping poison into them through two long, hollow teeth, called fangs. The end of a rattlesnake's tail is made up of horny segments. When the snake is threatened, it shakes its tail. This makes a loud, rattling noise and warns other animals to keep away.

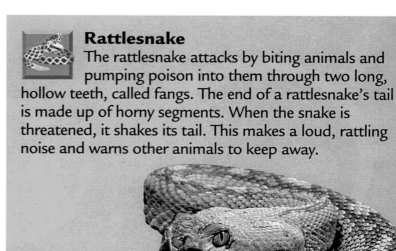

Florida Everglades

The Florida Everglades is a hot, steamy swamp where there are plenty of streams of running water. Strange **birds** dive for **fish**, and sleepy alligators doze in the tall grasses that line the shore. The **climate** is always warm and there are only two seasons, wet and dry.

Anhinga
The anhinga is also called a snakebird, because it often swims partly underwater, wriggling its long head and neck like a snake.

Tree frog
The small green tree frog is well **camouflaged** against the tree roots. It catches tasty **insects** with its long, sticky tongue.

Diamondback terrapin
The terrapin speeds through the water using its strong, webbed hind feet.

The tree frog has long toes that help it to climb through the trees. Sticky suction pads make it easy for the frog to grip smooth tree trunks and cling onto slippery leaves.

Female terrapins lay soft, leathery eggs in a hole on the shore. Several weeks later, baby terrapins hatch, dig their way out of the sand, and rush to the safety of the water.

Anhingas feed on fish and frogs, which they seize from the water with their long, daggerlike **bills**. They kill their **prey** by beating it against the ground. Then, they swallow it whole.

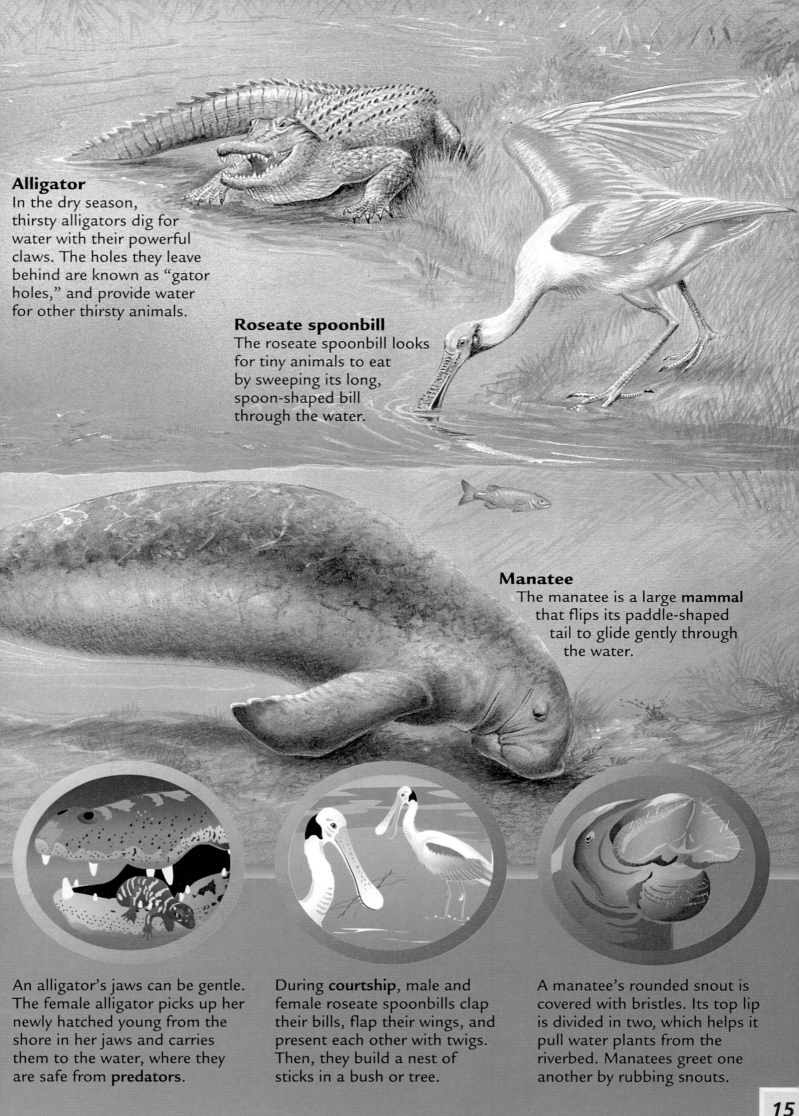

Alligator
In the dry season, thirsty alligators dig for water with their powerful claws. The holes they leave behind are known as "gator holes," and provide water for other thirsty animals.

Roseate spoonbill
The roseate spoonbill looks for tiny animals to eat by sweeping its long, spoon-shaped bill through the water.

Manatee
The manatee is a large **mammal** that flips its paddle-shaped tail to glide gently through the water.

An alligator's jaws can be gentle. The female alligator picks up her newly hatched young from the shore in her jaws and carries them to the water, where they are safe from **predators**.

During **courtship**, male and female roseate spoonbills clap their bills, flap their wings, and present each other with twigs. Then, they build a nest of sticks in a bush or tree.

A manatee's rounded snout is covered with bristles. Its top lip is divided in two, which helps it pull water plants from the riverbed. Manatees greet one another by rubbing snouts.

Mexico, Central America, and the Caribbean

Northern Mexico is a dry, mountainous desert. The animals here have **adapted** to the hot **climate,** finding special ways to keep cool and look for food and water. Southern Mexico and the rest of Central America are covered with thick, damp rain forest where bloodsucking bats, darting lizards, and giant spiders make their homes. The beautiful Caribbean Islands lie off Central America's eastern shore.

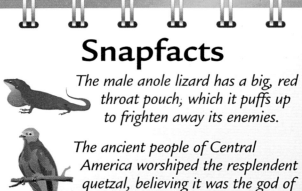

Snapfacts

The male anole lizard has a big, red throat pouch, which it puffs up to frighten away its enemies.

The ancient people of Central America worshiped the resplendent quetzal, believing it was the god of the air.

The Jesus Christ lizard is so small and light that it can run across rivers without falling in.

Kinkajou
The kinkajou is a member of the raccoon family. It spends most of its life in the trees, hanging from branches by its long tail. In the daytime, it rests in the hollow of a tree. The kinkajou is also called a honey bear because it sometimes raids bees' nests and eats the honey.

SIERRA MADRE

MEXICO

Gila woodpecker

Red-kneed tarantula

Monarch butterfly (go to p11)

Scarlet macaw

①

Hognose snake

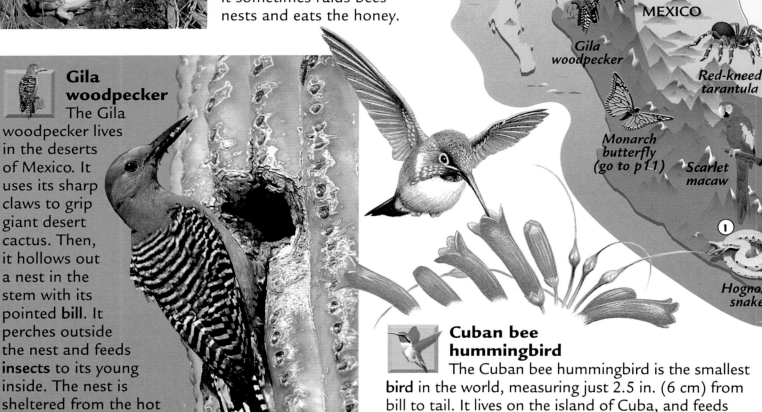

Gila woodpecker
The Gila woodpecker lives in the deserts of Mexico. It uses its sharp claws to grip giant desert cactus. Then, it hollows out a nest in the stem with its pointed **bill**. It perches outside the nest and feeds **insects** to its young inside. The nest is sheltered from the hot sun and is also well protected. Few animals want to climb a prickly cactus!

Cuban bee hummingbird
The Cuban bee hummingbird is the smallest **bird** in the world, measuring just 2.5 in. (6 cm) from bill to tail. It lives on the island of Cuba, and feeds on the **nectar** of flowers. Bee hummingbirds beat their wings so fast, up to 70 times a second, that they make a humming noise, just like a bee.

Ocelot

The ocelot is a wild cat that sleeps during the day and comes out to feed at night. It is also called a leopard cat. Ocelots are good climbers and swimmers. They hunt silently through the rain forest, catching small **mammals**, snakes, and birds. Ocelots are rare because their forest home is being destroyed, and they are hunted for their fur.

CAN YOU FIND...

❶ a snake that rolls over and pretends to be dead when it is threatened?

❷ a fast **fish** with a long, swordlike nose?

❸ a group of ferocious insects that attacks animals on the forest floor?

❹ a red bird with a long, curved bill?

❺ a bat that feeds on the blood of cattle and other animals?

Red-kneed tarantula

The red-kneed tarantula is a large, hairy spider that lives in a burrow in the ground. A female tarantula uses her front legs to seize any insects that come too close to the entrance of her burrow.

Scarlet macaw

Scarlet macaws live in flocks near the edge of the rain forest. These birds eat seeds and nuts, which they hold in their claws and split open with their strong, hooked bills. A macaw often uses its feet to pass food up to its mouth.

③ Army ants

Cuban bee hummingbird

Anole lizard

CENTRAL AMERICA

Resplendent quetzal

Kinkajou

② Swordfish

CARIBBEAN ISLANDS

⑤

Vampire bat

Caribbean Sea

④

Scarlet ibis

Jesus Christ lizard

N

W

E

S

Ocelot

South America

The landscape across South America varies greatly, from steamy, tropical rain forests in the north to cold, windswept islands in the far south. Bursting with noise and color, the rain forest is packed with screeching monkeys and **birds**. High mountains, dry deserts, and rolling grasslands, called pampas, also stretch across the South American **continent**.

Orinoco R.

Howler monk

GALAPAGOS ISLANDS
(go to p20-21)

②

Llama

Harpy eagle

Toucan
Toucans have enormous, brightly colored **bills** for sawing pieces out of large fruits. Some toucans also pick off small fruits with the tips of their bills, throw them into the air, and then catch them at the backs of their throats. A toucan's bill is not as heavy as it looks!

Snapfacts

An arrow-poison frog has enough deadly poison in its skin to kill 1,500 people.

Leaf-cutter ants can strip all the leaves from a bush in a single night.

The noisy howler monkey's screams can be heard almost 10 miles (16 km) away.

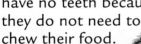

Giant anteater
The giant anteater has a keen **sense** of smell and is an expert at sniffing out ants and termites to eat. When an anteater finds an ants' or termites' nest, it rips it open with its strong front claws. Then, it shoots its long, sticky tongue into the nest and picks up hundreds of ants with one lick. Anteaters have no teeth because they do not need to chew their food.

Sloth
The sloth spends most of its time clinging to rain forest trees. It hooks its long claws around branches and holds on so tightly that it can even fall asleep in this position. Sloths move slowly, shifting one foot at a time.

Sloth

Jaguar

Equator

Amazon River

Piranhas

①

Leaf-cutter ants

Toucan

Amazon
Rainforest

São Francisco River

Arrow-poison
frog

⑤

Golden lion
tamarin

Pampas

③

Nine-banded
armadillo

Paraná River

Desert

N

E

W

S

ANDES MOUNTAINS

Giant
anteater

④

Fur seals

Harpy eagle

The harpy eagle is a fast and ferocious hunter that flies above the rain forest, looking for monkeys and other animals that live in the treetops. When it spies its **prey**, it dives through the branches and catches the animal with its huge, hooked talons. Harpy eagles are rare. They nest in the tallest trees, on giant platforms made of twigs.

CAN YOU FIND...

❶ a river **fish** that lives in big groups and attacks animals with its razor-sharp teeth?

❷ an animal that looks like a camel without a hump?

❸ a **mammal** whose body is covered with thick armor?

❹ a furry animal that lives in the icy southern ocean?

❺ a tiny monkey with a golden coat and a long, silky mane?

Jaguar

The jaguar is the largest wild cat in South America. It hunts birds, deer, and wild pigs. It also swims through rivers to catch fish. A jaguar's spotted coat helps to hide it in the dappled light of the forest so that it can creep up unseen on its prey.

Galapagos Islands

The Galapagos are a group of volcanic islands that lie off South America's west coast. These rocky, barren islands are so remote that strange animals have **evolved** here, including giant land and sea **reptiles**, and unusual kinds of **birds**. Most animals live on the coast, where food is plentiful.

Galapagos penguin

Most penguins live near icy Antarctica. But the Galapagos penguins live near the warm Equator. They can survive here because of a cold water current that flows up from Antarctica.

Marine iguana

The marine iguana is the only lizard that lives in the sea. Its long claws help it to climb onto the rocks, where it warms its body in the sun.

Sally-lightfoot crab

During the day, sally-lightfoot crabs hide in cracks and crevices in the rocks. At night, they come out to feed in large numbers.

The marine iguana can hold its breath for almost an hour while it grazes underwater on seaweed-covered rocks. When it returns to the surface, it blows out a shower of water and fills its lungs with air.

The sally-lightfoot crab clings to the rock face as huge waves crash over it and onto the shore. The crab scuttles sideways across the ground, feeding on seaweed and dead iguanas.

Like all penguins, Galapagos penguins cannot fly. But their smooth, sleek bodies and stiff, stubby wings help them to chase **fish** through the water at great speeds.

Magnificent frigate bird
The magnificent frigate bird's long, narrow wings help it to glide over the ocean and swoop down to the water at great speed.

Giant tortoise
The giant tortoise's shell is over 3 feet (1 m) long. Some kinds of giant tortoise have arched shells, so that the tortoises can stretch up their long necks and feed on tender leaves.

Blue-footed booby
The blue-footed booby lays its eggs on open ground. Both parents take turns keeping the eggs warm by covering them with their broad, webbed feet.

The male magnificent frigate bird has a special way of attracting a female. During **courtship**, he blows up the bright red pouch on his throat so that it looks like an enormous red balloon.

In the **mating season**, the male blue-footed booby performs a special walk, lifting and showing off his dazzling, blue feet. He also performs a flying display for his **mate**, flashing his feet as he lands.

Ticks feed on the skin under a giant tortoise's shell. Small birds help tortoises to get rid of these tiny pests by climbing underneath their shells and feeding on them.

Northern Europe

Northern Europe is a cool, wet area with thick evergreen forests in the north, and rolling woodlands and fields in the south. Many small **mammals** live here. Large groups, or colonies, of sea birds nest along the deserted northern coast.

Wolverine

Arctic Circle

Ermine
(go to p8)

Reindeer
(go to p26)

③ Osprey

Puffin
ICELAND

② Red deer

Red squirrel

Badger

Elbe River

Otters

Wild boar

N

Seine River

W   E

Stag beetle

④ Hedgehog

Red fox

S

Loire River

①

Danube River

⑤ Kingfisher

Northern viper

🔭 CAN YOU FIND...

❶ a **reptile** with a poisonous bite that slithers along the ground?

❷ an animal with antlers, long legs, and a reddish-brown coat?

❸ a large **bird** that plunges feet-first into rivers and catches **fish** with its talons?

❹ a prickly animal that rolls up into a tight ball when it feels threatened?

❺ one of the most brightly colored birds in Europe, that lives by rivers and lakes?

Red squirrel
The red squirrel is perfectly suited to life in the forest. It is light enough to leap from tree to tree, gripping the branches with its sharp claws. In autumn, the red squirrel buries a store of nuts and seeds, and builds a snug nest where it sleeps on cold days.

Otter

This playful mammal lives in clean, quiet rivers. Its long, sleek body and webbed feet make it an expert swimmer. Otters are ferocious hunters, diving and swooping as they chase fish through the water. They live in underground dens that they dig out under the roots of trees along the riverbanks.

Red fox

The red fox is a member of the dog family. This cunning, bold animal is a skillful hunter. It catches rabbits, birds, and other small animals in fields and woods close to its home. Foxes have **adapted** well to life in towns. Many live in gardens and parks and are often spotted raiding garbage cans for food.

Wolverine

The wolverine is a swift and powerful animal with sharp teeth and a crushing bite. It can kill animals that are larger than itself, such as reindeer. When it cannot find food, it may force wolves or bears to share their meat. It has a thick fur coat that keeps it warm in winter.

Snapfacts

The badger lives in an underground den, called a sett, that can have tunnels as long as tennis courts.

The wild boar is excellent at sniffing out food. It can easily find roots and bulbs that are buried deep underground.

The male stag beetle has huge jaws that look like antlers. It uses them to fight other male stag beetles.

Puffin

This small sea bird spends most of its time fishing in the open sea. It dives into the water and packs several small fish into its bright, striped **bill**. In spring, puffins gather in huge noisy colonies and nest on cliffs along the coast. They lay their eggs in burrows to keep them safe from other hungry sea birds.

Southern Europe

Southern Europe is warm, sunny, and mostly dry. Rocky hills and **scrubland** cover much of the land, and are home to all kinds of **birds** and small **reptiles**. There are also two huge, snowy mountain ranges: the Alps and the Pyrenees. The mammals that live here are sure-footed, and have thick fur coats to keep them warm.

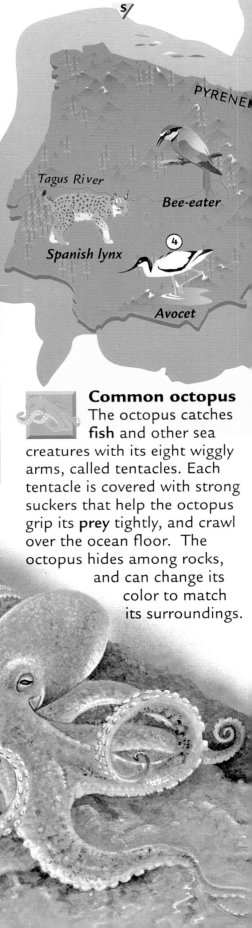

PYRENE

Tagus River

Spanish lynx

Bee-eater

Avocet

4

Fire salamander
The fire salamander is an **amphibian** with bright yellow markings on its body that warn other animals that it is poisonous. Most salamanders live on land in rotten logs, under rocks, and in other cool, dark places.

Common octopus
The octopus catches **fish** and other sea creatures with its eight wiggly arms, called tentacles. Each tentacle is covered with strong suckers that help the octopus grip its **prey** tightly, and crawl over the ocean floor. The octopus hides among rocks, and can change its color to match its surroundings.

CAN YOU FIND...

❶ an intelligent and friendly sea **mammal** that swims behind boats and can leap out of the water high into the air?

❷ a small animal that lives on mountain slopes, and is a relative of the squirrel?

❸ a slow-moving reptile whose hard shell protects it from the hot sun?

❹ a shore bird with a long, curved **bill** that visits southern Europe in summer to nest and **breed**?

❺ a sea mammal that is one of the rarest of its kind in the world?

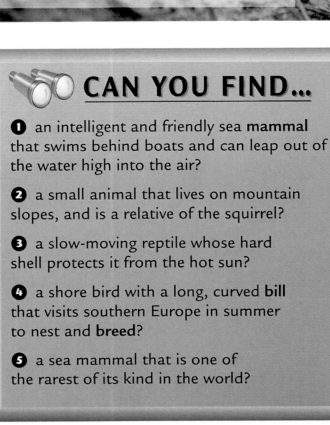

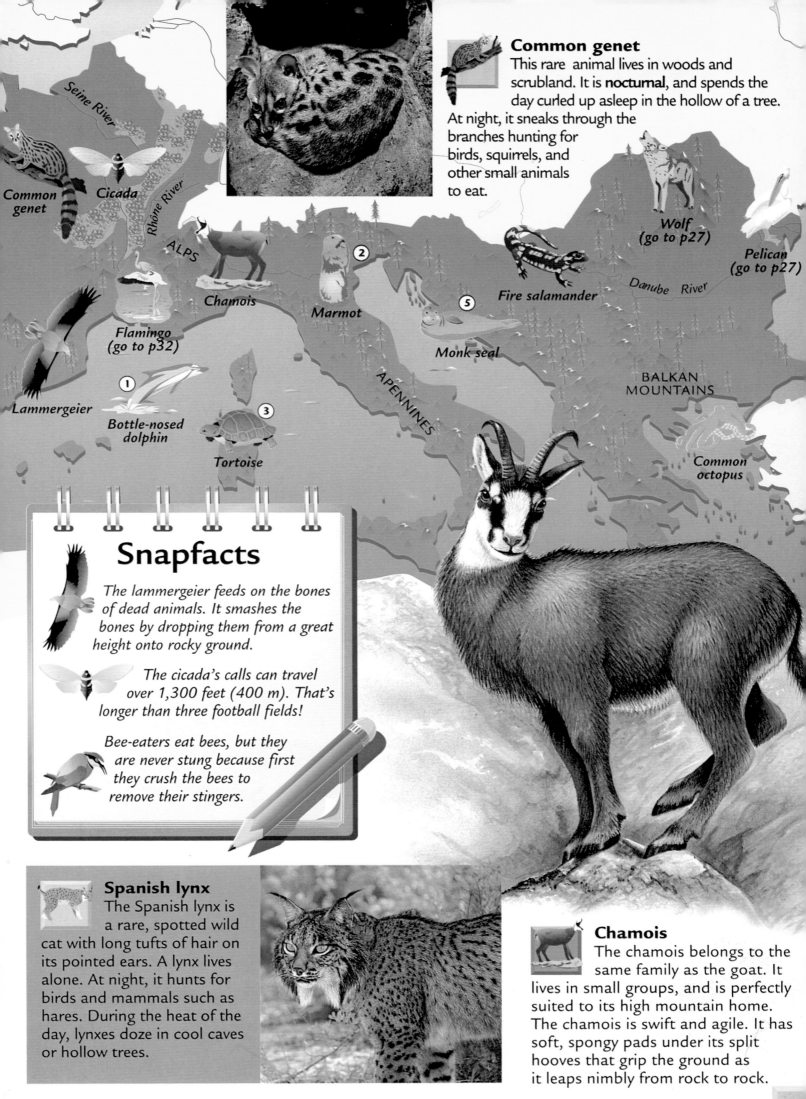

Seine River

Rhône River

Common genet

Cicada

ALPS

Chamois

Flamingo (go to p32)

Lammergeier

Bottle-nosed dolphin

Tortoise

Marmot

APENNINES

Monk seal

Fire salamander

Danube River

Wolf (go to p27)

Pelican (go to p27)

BALKAN MOUNTAINS

Common octopus

Common genet

This rare animal lives in woods and scrubland. It is **nocturnal**, and spends the day curled up asleep in the hollow of a tree. At night, it sneaks through the branches hunting for birds, squirrels, and other small animals to eat.

Snapfacts

The lammergeier feeds on the bones of dead animals. It smashes the bones by dropping them from a great height onto rocky ground.

The cicada's calls can travel over 1,300 feet (400 m). That's longer than three football fields!

Bee-eaters eat bees, but they are never stung because first they crush the bees to remove their stingers.

Spanish lynx

The Spanish lynx is a rare, spotted wild cat with long tufts of hair on its pointed ears. A lynx lives alone. At night, it hunts for birds and mammals such as hares. During the heat of the day, lynxes doze in cool caves or hollow trees.

Chamois

The chamois belongs to the same family as the goat. It lives in small groups, and is perfectly suited to its high mountain home. The chamois is swift and agile. It has soft, spongy pads under its split hooves that grip the ground as it leaps nimbly from rock to rock.

Russia and its neighbors

Russia and its neighboring countries stretch almost halfway around the top of the Earth. The land is made up of snaking mountain ranges, windswept grasslands, frozen **tundra,** and the largest forest in the world, called the taiga. During the long winter, the weather is cold and harsh, and food is scarce. Many animals **hibernate** or travel south to warmer parts of the world.

Reindeer

In summer, reindeer graze on grasses and mosses. In winter, they kick away the snow with their sharp hooves to find lichens and other small plants to eat. When food is scarce, reindeer may gather in huge herds and **migrate**.

Hamster

Lemming

Arctic Circle

Don River

URAL MOUNTAINS

Ob River

Black Sea

Pelican

Volga River

Waxwing

④

③

Irtysh River

Wolf

Caspian Sea

Edible frog

Sturgeon

Aral Sea

Kara Kum Desert

Amu Darya River

Snapfacts

The Baikal seal is one of the few seals to live in **fresh water**.

The sturgeon is a **fish** whose eggs are eaten as a delicacy all over the world. The eggs are known as caviar.

Each winter, the east Siberian willow warbler flies an incredible 7,800 miles (13,000 km) to eastern Africa.

Hamster

During the day, the hamster snoozes in an underground burrow. At night, it comes out to search for roots and seeds, which it keeps in large pouches inside its cheeks. The hamster takes the food back to its burrow and stores it here to eat during the cold winter months.

Moose
(go to p10)

Reindeer

Mosquito

East Siberian
willow warbler

Yenisey River

Lena River

Brown bear

Siberian tiger

Taiga

YABLONOVYY
MOUNTAINS

Amur River

Baikal seal

Lake
Baikal

Siberian tiger
The Siberian tiger is the world's largest cat. It has a thick, shaggy coat that keeps it warm in winter. Siberian tigers are very rare. They live alone and stalk wild boar and deer. Tigers mark their territory by leaving **scent** droppings, and scraping marks on trees with their sharp claws. They warn off other tigers with a fierce roar.

CAN YOU FIND...

❶ a small animal with sharp front teeth that feeds on seeds on the tundra?

❷ a flying **insect** that can infect humans with a deadly illness called malaria?

❸ a green, speckly animal that lives on land but returns to the water to **breed**?

❹ a **bird** that is named after the red spots on its wings, which look like melted wax?

❺ a large forest animal that is related to the Canadian grizzly bear?

Pelican
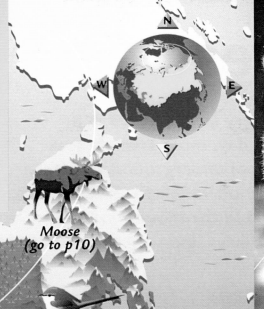
The pelican is a large waterbird that is an expert at catching fish. It ducks its head underwater and scoops up its food in a baggy pouch under its **bill**. Then, it lifts its head, lets the water stream out of its bill, and feasts on its catch.

Wolf
Most wolves live in family groups called packs. Each wolf holds a different position, or rank, in the pack. When two wolves meet, they immediately let each other know their rank. The high-ranking wolf stands up straight, raises its tail in the air, and pricks up its ears. The low-ranking wolf crouches and lowers its tail and ears.

Southwest Asia

Southwest Asia is a hot, dry land covered with sandy desert. During the day, most animals seek shelter from the sun in cool underground burrows. These animals can survive on very little water. Along the coast, in river valleys, and in the mountains, water is more plentiful. Here, monkeys and wild cats are found.

Praying mantis

①

Desert locust

②

Sacred baboon

Red Sea

Dromedary camel

The dromedary camel is perfectly **adapted** to desert life. The hump on its back contains a store of fat that helps it survive for days without water or food. In sandstorms, its long, curly eyelashes keep sand out of its eyes, and its nostrils close tightly to stop sand from blowing up its nose.

Desert jerboa

The desert jerboa drinks little water, and feeds on dry grass and seeds. It spends the hot days in a deep, cool burrow, only coming out when the sun has set. The jerboa has strong back legs and can hop away from danger, like a kangaroo.

CAN YOU FIND...

❶ a flying insect that gathers in huge swarms, eating all the plants and crops that lie in its path?

❷ a big monkey that moves on all fours, and lives and hunts on the ground?

❸ a giant lizard that feeds on **birds** and rats and will even eat its own young?

❹ a desert animal with huge ears that help to keep it cool?

❺ a snake that buries itself in the sand to shelter from the desert sun?

Praying mantis

The praying mantis hides on plants, waiting to pounce on **insects**. When one lands nearby, the mantis keeps absolutely still and stares at its victim with its huge eyes. Then, it shoots out its two long front legs, snatches its **prey**, and quickly tears it apart.

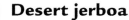

④

Fennec fox ELBURZ MOUNTAINS

Tigris River

uphrates River

ZAGROS MOUNTAINS

Leopard

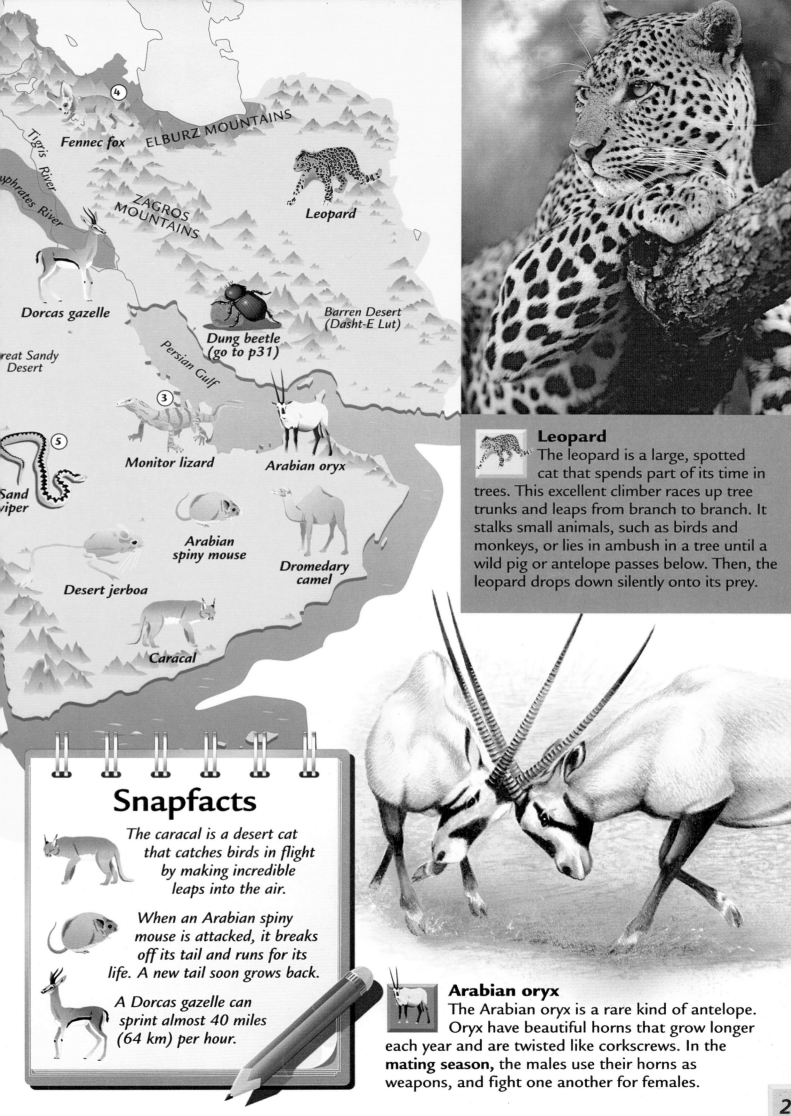

Dorcas gazelle

reat Sandy Desert

Dung beetle (go to p31)

Persian Gulf

Barren Desert (Dasht-E Lut)

③

⑤

Sand viper

Monitor lizard

Arabian oryx

Arabian spiny mouse

Dromedary camel

Desert jerboa

Caracal

Leopard
The leopard is a large, spotted cat that spends part of its time in trees. This excellent climber races up tree trunks and leaps from branch to branch. It stalks small animals, such as birds and monkeys, or lies in ambush in a tree until a wild pig or antelope passes below. Then, the leopard drops down silently onto its prey.

Snapfacts

The caracal is a desert cat that catches birds in flight by making incredible leaps into the air.

When an Arabian spiny mouse is attacked, it breaks off its tail and runs for its life. A new tail soon grows back.

A Dorcas gazelle can sprint almost 40 miles (64 km) per hour.

Arabian oryx
The Arabian oryx is a rare kind of antelope. Oryx have beautiful horns that grow longer each year and are twisted like corkscrews. In the **mating season**, the males use their horns as weapons, and fight one another for females.

2

Northern Africa

The baking-hot Sahara, which is the largest desert on Earth, covers most of northern Africa. Many of the animals here are **nocturnal**, coming out to feed only in the cool of the night. South of the Sahara, there is a large area of grasses and scattered trees, where some of the world's largest **mammals** roam.

White rhinoceros
The white rhinoceros has such a broad snout that Dutch settlers gave it the name "weid." This means "wide," but has been wrongly translated as "white." A white rhinoceros has two curved horns made of densely packed hair. It lives peacefully, grazing on grass and wallowing in cool, muddy pools.

ATLAS MOUNTAINS

Barbary sheep ⑤

④ **Scorpion**

Sahara Desert

AHAGGAR MOUNTAINS

① **Spotted hyena**

③ **Pangolin**

Chimpanzees (go to p32) *Lake Volta*

Red-billed quelea

Secretary bird

CAN YOU FIND...

❶ an animal with bone-crushing jaws that hunts in packs and also steals meat from other animals?

❷ a flying **insect** that infects people and cattle with a dangerous disease called sleeping sickness?

❸ an animal that can roll itself tightly into a ball, and whose body is covered with protective scales?

❹ a relative of the spider that lives in the desert, and has a poisonous stinger in its tail?

❺ a long-horned member of the goat family that lives in the desert?

African elephant

The African elephant is the world's largest land animal. Its long, sensitive trunk is really a nose and top lip joined together. The elephant uses its trunk to breathe, smell, and wash itself, as well as to drink and eat, to trumpet loudly, and even to spank its young.

Oxpecker

Flocks of oxpeckers live alongside other animals, such as crocodiles. They scuttle over a crocodile's body, pecking at the fleas, ticks, and maggots that live on its back, head, and teeth. The crocodile cannot remove these tiny pests itself, so it lets the oxpeckers do the job instead!

Secretary bird

The secretary **bird** has long, strong legs and a sharp, hooked **bill**. It hunts snakes, rats, and lizards, which it pins to the ground with its feet and stamps to death. Its name comes from the feathers on its head, which look like the quills that secretaries once used as pens.

Dromedary camel (go to p28)

Nile River

Nile crocodile

Red Sea

Dung beetle

②

Tsetse fly

White rhino

Oxpecker

Cheetah

African elephant

East Siberian willow warbler (go to p26)

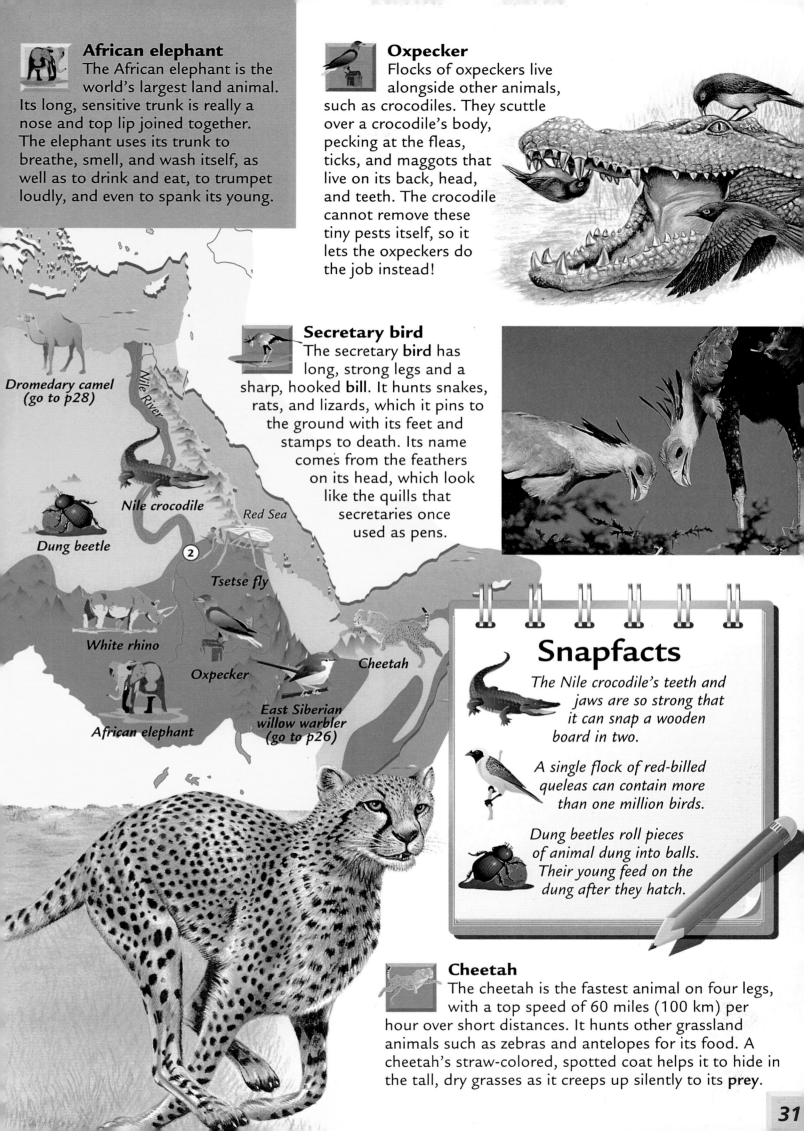

Snapfacts

The Nile crocodile's teeth and jaws are so strong that it can snap a wooden board in two.

A single flock of red-billed queleas can contain more than one million birds.

Dung beetles roll pieces of animal dung into balls. Their young feed on the dung after they hatch.

Cheetah

The cheetah is the fastest animal on four legs, with a top speed of 60 miles (100 km) per hour over short distances. It hunts other grassland animals such as zebras and antelopes for its food. A cheetah's straw-colored, spotted coat helps it to hide in the tall, dry grasses as it creeps up silently to its **prey**.

Southern Africa

Near southern Africa's Great Rift Valley is an area of vast grassy plains called the savannah. Here, large herds of animals graze and search for water holes, trying to avoid fierce **predators** such as lions. Southern Africa has a varied landscape, with dense tropical rain forests, rocky mountains, and dry deserts stretching across the land. Many of southern Africa's animals now live in large protected parks called game reserves.

Meerkat

Meerkats live underneath the plains in burrows with many tunnels. They feed on **insects**, spiders, and even scorpions. One meerkat stands guard, while the others dig food out of the ground. When a meerkat catches a scorpion, it first bites off its tail and deadly poisonous stinger.

Gorilla

The gorilla is the largest member of the ape family. Fully grown, it can weigh more than two people. Gorillas live in family groups on mountains and in forests, where they feed on juicy fruits and leaves. When a gorilla is born, it is tiny and weak. It stays close to its mother until it is about 3 years old.

Lion

Lions are powerful cats with sharp teeth and huge, padded paws. They live in large groups called prides. Each pride has several female lions, called lionesses, their young cubs, and a few males. Lionesses share the job of looking after the cubs. They also hunt and kill other animals for the pride to eat, while the males guard the home.

CAN YOU FIND...

❶ a long-legged **bird** that gathers in huge flocks around **saltwater** lakes?

❷ a member of the ape family that uses its strong arms to swing through the trees?

❸ a snake that first bites its **prey**, then swallows it whole?

❹ a small bird that builds a big, round nest to attract female birds?

❺ an insect that is the heaviest in the world and weighs as much as a mouse?

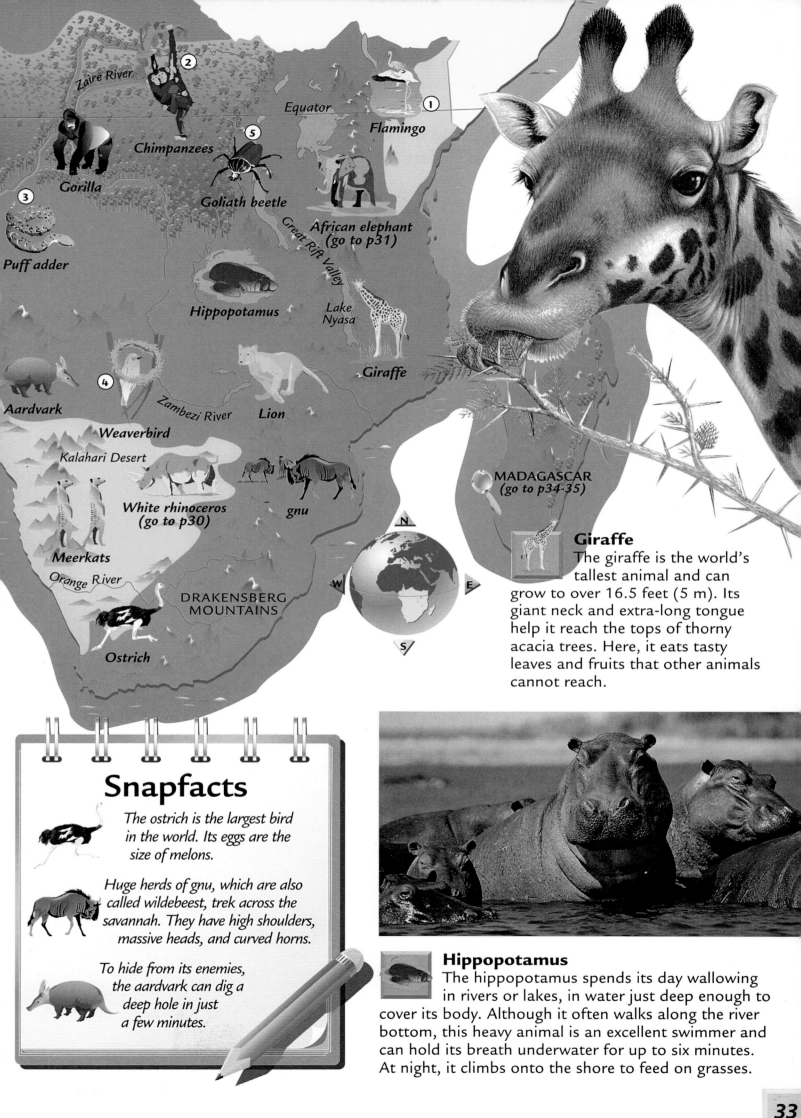

Zaire River

② Chimpanzees

Gorilla

③ Puff adder

④ Aardvark

Weaverbird

Kalahari Desert

Meerkats

Orange River

DRAKENSBERG MOUNTAINS

Ostrich

Equator

① Flamingo

⑤ Goliath beetle

African elephant (go to p31)

Great Rift Valley

Hippopotamus

Lake Nyasa

Giraffe

Zambezi River

Lion

White rhinoceros (go to p30)

gnu

MADAGASCAR (go to p34-35)

N
W   E
S

Giraffe
The giraffe is the world's tallest animal and can grow to over 16.5 feet (5 m). Its giant neck and extra-long tongue help it reach the tops of thorny acacia trees. Here, it eats tasty leaves and fruits that other animals cannot reach.

Snapfacts

The ostrich is the largest bird in the world. Its eggs are the size of melons.

Huge herds of gnu, which are also called wildebeest, trek across the savannah. They have high shoulders, massive heads, and curved horns.

To hide from its enemies, the aardvark can dig a deep hole in just a few minutes.

Hippopotamus
The hippopotamus spends its day wallowing in rivers or lakes, in water just deep enough to cover its body. Although it often walks along the river bottom, this heavy animal is an excellent swimmer and can hold its breath underwater for up to six minutes. At night, it climbs onto the shore to feed on grasses.

Madagascar

Madagascar is the fourth largest island in the world. It has lush, tropical rain forests where monkeylike animals, called lemurs, chatter and screech, leaping through the treetops with acrobatic skill. Near the ground, **reptiles** lie **camouflaged**, waiting for juicy **insects** to land nearby.

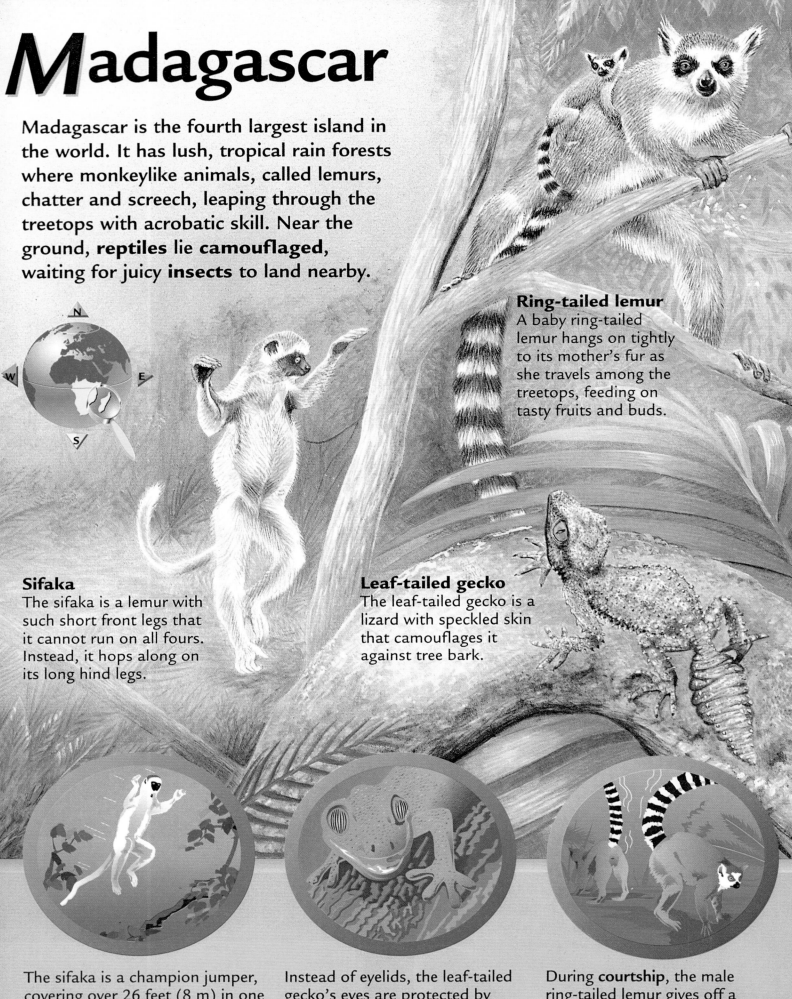

Ring-tailed lemur
A baby ring-tailed lemur hangs on tightly to its mother's fur as she travels among the treetops, feeding on tasty fruits and buds.

Sifaka
The sifaka is a lemur with such short front legs that it cannot run on all fours. Instead, it hops along on its long hind legs.

Leaf-tailed gecko
The leaf-tailed gecko is a lizard with speckled skin that camouflages it against tree bark.

The sifaka is a champion jumper, covering over 26 feet (8 m) in one leap. It kicks off backward from a tree, twists around in mid-air, and lands facing forward on another tree.

Instead of eyelids, the leaf-tailed gecko's eyes are protected by a clear, rigid covering. To clean its eyes and keep them moist, the gecko licks them with its long, sticky tongue.

During **courtship**, the male ring-tailed lemur gives off a strong **scent** under its arms, which it wipes onto its tail. Then, the male has a "stink fight" by waving its tail at rival males.

Aye-aye
The aye-aye is a lemur whose front teeth never stop growing. It gnaws on wood and hard fruits that wear down its teeth.

Fossa
The fossa is the largest **predator** on Madagascar. This catlike animal hunts at night, pouncing on its **prey** of lemurs and **birds**.

Common chameleon
The chameleon's tongue is as long as its body. This lizard shoots out its tongue and catches insects on its club-shaped, sticky tip.

The fossa's sharp claws are similar to the spikes on a climber's boots. They dig into tree bark so that the animal can walk down a tree head-first. The fossa can also pull in its claws like a cat.

Each one of the chameleon's eyes can swivel on its own, to look backward, forward, up, or down. This means that it can see in two directions at once, and is more likely to spot juicy prey.

The aye-aye has such good hearing that it can pick up the faint sound of insects under tree bark. It then digs under the bark with its long, bony finger and pulls out the insects to eat.

Southern Asia

Southern Asia stretches from the high, snow-capped mountains of the Himalaya in the north to parched deserts in the west. In the south, there are wide rivers and valleys, tropical rain forests, and open plains. Many of the different kinds of animals that live in southern Asia, such as rhinoceroses and elephants, are also found on the African grasslands.

Helmand River

Indus Ri...

② *Ratel*

Mongoo...
Thar Desert

①

Asian wild ass

Snapfacts

The mongoose moves so quickly that it can bite a snake on the back of its head.

An Asian elephant can carry a 600-lb (270-kg) log in its trunk, which is the same weight as lifting eight children.

After giving birth, the tree shrew visits her young only once every two days.

King cobra
The king cobra can grow over 16.5 feet (5 m) long. It is the world's longest poisonous snake. When the king cobra is threatened, it raises the front of its body and spreads out the skin on the side of its neck to form a hood. This makes it look more frightening to its enemies.

Tiger
Tigers have striped coats that **camouflage** them from their **prey**. They are the largest and strongest members of the cat family. Tigers stalk animals such as buffalo, deer, and pigs, but they can also swim and catch **fish**. In 1970, tigers became protected animals. Since then, the number of wild tigers has doubled. However, they are still rare. Smaller numbers of tigers are also found in other parts of Asia.

CAN YOU FIND...

❶ an animal that looks similar to a donkey but can run as fast as a horse?

❷ a member of the badger family that raids bees' nests to feed on honey?

❸ a large animal with a thick, bumpy skin that looks like a suit of armor?

❹ an ox-like animal that lives in bamboo forests in the Himalaya?

❺ a **reptile** with a long, narrow snout?

Snow leopard

N

W · E

S

④ Takin

HIMALAYA

③ Indian rhinoceros

King cobra

Ganges River

Asian elephant

Brahmaputra River

⑤ Gharial

armada River

Blue Peacock

Atlas moth

Tiger

Tree shrew

Water buffalo

Robber crab (go to p41)

Atlas moth

The giant atlas moth measures up to 12 in. (30 cm) from wing tip to wing tip. On its wings, it has brightly colored spots and markings. These distract the moth's enemies, such as birds, and may stop them from attacking its head.

Snow leopard

The snow leopard lives high in the Himalaya. It has a thick, pale gray coat that keeps it warm and is marked with brown spots that help it to hide from its prey. This rare and powerful animal leaps over ravines and climbs steep, icy slopes as it hunts for wild sheep and goats.

Blue peacock

In the **mating season**, the male blue peacock attracts a female by displaying its magnificent feathers in a shimmering fan and parading slowly in front of her. The feathers, called a train, are five times as long as the **bird**'s body.

Water buffalo

The water buffalo is a powerful animal with large, curved horns. Water buffalo live in herds in the marshes of southern Asia. During the hottest part of the day, they wade into the river for a cool dip. Water buffalo are fearless. They will even threaten a tiger by snorting, stamping, and lowering their horns.

Eastern Asia

Eastern Asia is a vast land with many contrasting habitats. On the high, icy plains of the snow-covered Himalaya, shaggy-haired cattle search for food. Rare animals such as pandas make their homes in the thick bamboo forests, alligators swim in the flowing rivers, and antelope graze the windy grasslands. Hardy camels and horses roam the harsh northern deserts.

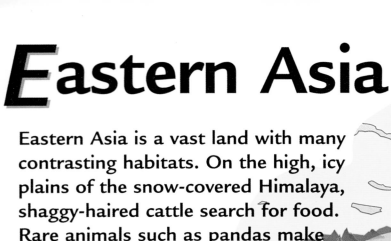

Przewalski's horse

Asian wild ass (go to p36)

Bactrian camel

Gobi Desert

Takla Makan Desert

⑤

Saiga

②

Yak

HIMALAYA

④

Golden pheasant

N

W

E

S

①

Red panda

Giant panda

Giant pandas are very rare and are found in the wild only in this part of the world. The giant panda's favorite food is bamboo, which grows in cool mountain forests. This shy animal has developed an extra pad on its front paws to grasp the bamboo shoots as it chews.

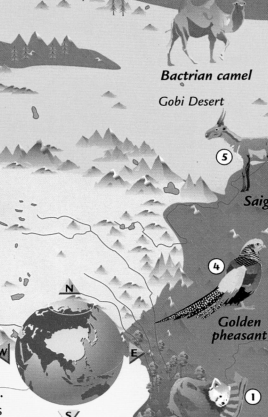

Chinese river dolphin

The Chinese river dolphin is one of the few dolphins that lives in **fresh water**. The rivers where it swims are often muddy and **polluted**, and the dolphin's eyesight is poor. To find its way around, it makes high-pitched noises that bounce off objects nearby and send echoes back to its ears. The echoes help the dolphin to catch **fish** and avoid large obstacles, such as boats.

Japanese crane

Japanese cranes are rare, beautiful **birds**. A male and female stay together for life, and raise a new family each year. Before they **mate**, the two birds perform an elegant **courtship** dance. They wave their heads, flap their wings, and leap into the air.

Japanese crane

Japanese macaque

Fish owl

Giant salamander

③

Yellow River

Chinese alligator

ngtze River

Chinese river dolphin

Giant panda

Japanese macaque

Japanese macaques live farther north than any other kind of monkey. Many make their homes high on volcanic mountains. To keep warm, they sit in hot springs that bubble up from under the ground. Macaques gather in large groups and feed on **insects**, nuts, and fruit.

Fish owl

The fish owl nests on river banks, and feeds mainly on fish. It hunts at night, snatching its wriggling **prey** from the water and gripping it tightly with its long, curved talons. The owl then carries the fish back to its perch to eat it. In winter, when the river freezes over, fish owls hunt squirrels, birds, and voles.

CAN YOU FIND...

❶ a forest animal with a red coat and a bushy tail with rings similar to a raccoon's?

❷ a large animal that lives in the mountains, and charges furiously when threatened?

❸ a relative of the crocodile that lives in rivers and marshes?

❹ a rare forest bird with a golden head and brilliant red feathers?

❺ a large-nosed member of the antelope family that lives in herds on the grasslands?

Snapfacts

*The giant salamander is the world's largest **amphibian**. It can grow up to 5 feet (1.5 m) long, which is about the length of a bicycle.*

Przewalski's horse was discovered only about 100 years ago.

The Bactrian camel is different from the dromedary—it has two humps instead of one.

Southeast Asia

Southeast Asia is made up of a narrow strip of mainland and thousands of islands scattered across the Indian and Pacific oceans. The weather here is warm and wet all year around, and thick, damp rain forests cover much of the land. The islands are alive with strange-looking monkeys, giant lizards, and swooping bats, and unusual **fish** dart through the surrounding water.

Estuarine crocodile

Kitti's hog-nosed bat

Flying gecko

Indian Ocean

Robber crab

Mekong River

Flower mantis

Malayan tapir

Proboscis monkey
The male proboscis monkey has a big pot belly and a long nose, about twice the size of a person's nose. When the monkey becomes excited, its nose turns red and grows larger, which helps him to attract a **mate**. Proboscis monkeys are rare. They are found only on one island, where they live in tall trees along the riverbanks.

Komodo dragon
The Komodo dragon is the world's largest lizard, and grows up to 10 feet (3 m) long. This massive animal eats meat and uses its sharp **sense** of smell and great strength to hunt monkeys, deer, and pigs. From time to time, it attacks humans. People have died after being bitten by a Komodo dragon because its saliva contains lots of germs.

Snapfacts

The estuarine crocodile can grow up to 20 feet (6 m) long and is the world's largest crocodile.

Kitti's hog-nosed bat is the smallest **mammal** in the world. Its wingspan is no wider than your hand.

The mudskipper is a strange fish. It leaves the water to feed on creatures on the muddy shore.

Flower mantis

The flower mantis is almost impossible to see against rain forest flowers. This is because the shape and color of the **insect's** body **camouflage** it perfectly, and make it look just like a petal. As soon as an insect lands on the flower, the mantis shoots out its two hooked arms and grabs hold of its **prey**.

Orangutan

The orangutan is a rare, red-haired ape. It grips the trees tightly with its jointed fingers, and swings from branch to branch, moving one hand after the other. Orangutans live alone and build a fresh, leafy nest to sleep in every night.

South China Sea

① Manta ray

② Dugong

North Pacific Ocean

Mudskipper

Proboscis monkey

Equator

⑤ Tree kangaroo

Orangutan

Sumatran tiger (go to p37)

Komodo dragon

Malayan tapir

The Malayan tapir is a hoofed animal that is about the size of a pony. It has strong black and white markings on its coat that help it to hide in the light and shade of the forest. Tapirs are timid animals. They feed mainly at night, using their long, flexible snouts to pull tender leaves and fruits from forest plants.

CAN YOU FIND...

❶ a large, flat fish that swims by lashing its tail and flapping its huge, winglike fins?

❷ an **endangered** sea mammal that looks like a seal and feeds only on plants?

❸ a small lizard that can glide from one tree to another?

❹ a crab that lives in muddy swamps along the coast and feeds on coconuts?

❺ a relative of the kangaroo that lives among the trees of the rain forest?

41

Australia, New Zealand, and the Pacific Islands

Australia and New Zealand are famous for their unusual **wildlife**. Kangaroos, kiwis, koalas, and many other animals are found only in this part of the world. This is because these countries, and many of the islands surrounding them, have been separated from the rest of the world for millions of years. During this time, the animals here have **evolved** in unique ways.

Snapfacts

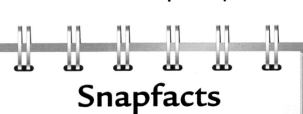

Tuataras are related to a group of **reptiles** that lived at the same time as the dinosaurs. Tuataras can live for up to 120 years.

The emu is a large, flightless **bird**. It can run at speeds of up to 30 miles (48 km) per hour.

The funnel-web spider is as small as your toe, but its bite is deadly.

Emu

AUSTRALIA

Echidna

Red kangaroos

Great Victoria Desert

Frilled liza

(5)

Numbat

(3)

Taipan

Funnel-
spide

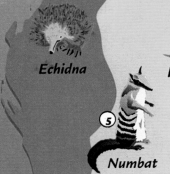

Koala

The koala is a bearlike animal that spends its time in the treetops. During the day, it sleeps wedged in the crook of a tree. In the late afternoon and at night, the koala feeds on eucalyptus leaves, which is the only food it eats. Koalas have long fingers and toes to grip tree branches, and sharp claws to cling to the trunks. They were once hunted for their soft, gray fur, but they are now protected by law.

Frilled lizard

The frilled lizard has an unusual way of defending itself. When it feels threatened, the animal opens its mouth and hisses. Then, a frill of skin expands and lies like a huge collar around its neck. This makes the lizard look bigger, and scares its enemies away.

Bird of paradise

N

W E

S

GREAT BARRIER REEF *(go to p44-45)*

GREAT DIVIDING RANGE

Koala

Darling River

①

Wombat

Murray River

Tasmanian devil

PACIFIC ISLANDS

Echidna

The echidna has a pointed snout to sniff out ants' nests, and a long, sticky tongue to slurp up the ants! This spiny-coated animal is a **mammal**, but instead of carrying its young inside its body, it lays eggs. After hatching, a baby echidna stays close to its mother until its own spines have grown.

CAN YOU FIND...

❶ a marsupial that looks like a bear, and digs deep burrows underground?

❷ a flightless bird with a long beak that sniffs out worms in the ground?

❸ a reptile that injects a deadly poison through a pair of long fangs?

❹ a bird whose beautiful tail feathers help it to win a **mate**?

❺ a large, ratlike animal with a striped body and a bushy tail?

NEW ZEALAND

Tuatara

②

Kiwi

Red kangaroo

The red kangaroo lives in herds called mobs. The female kangaroo gives birth to her young while it is still very tiny. The baby, called a joey, crawls into a pouch on its mother's body. It stays here for 6 months, feeding on its mother's milk and growing. Animals that have a pouch for their young to grow in are called marsupials.

Tasmanian devil

The Tasmanian devil earns its name from its black coloring and its strange, whining snarl. It hunts mainly at night, searching for small mammals and reptiles. During the day, it rests in a cave or hollow log.

Great Barrier Reef

The Great Barrier Reef is a large collection of **coral reefs** built by tiny animals called polyps. Coral reefs are found in warm, sunlit seas and are teeming with a rich variety of **wildlife**, from graceful sea anemones and groups of brightly colored **fish**, to prickly starfish and fierce sharks.

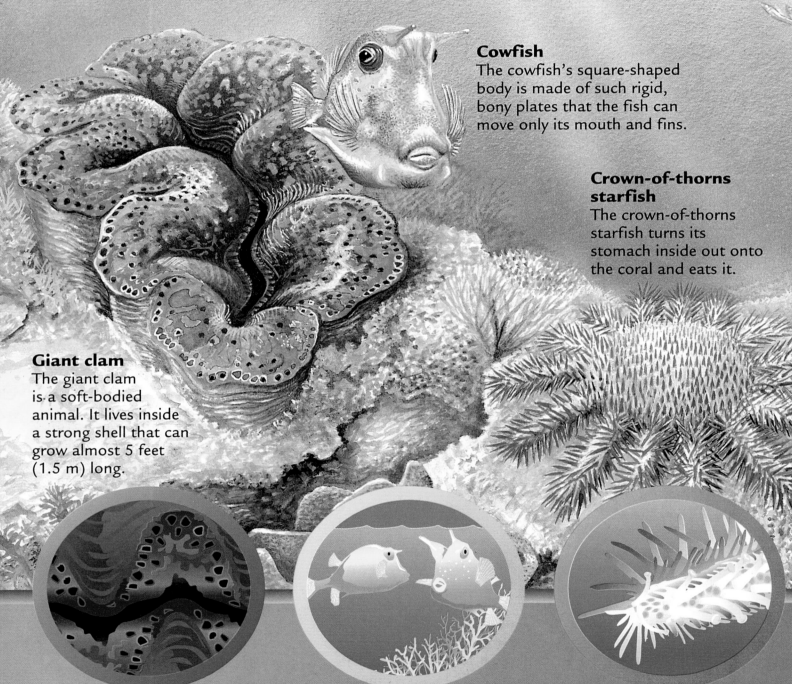

Cowfish

The cowfish's square-shaped body is made of such rigid, bony plates that the fish can move only its mouth and fins.

Crown-of-thorns starfish

The crown-of-thorns starfish turns its stomach inside out onto the coral and eats it.

Giant clam

The giant clam is a soft-bodied animal. It lives inside a strong shell that can grow almost 5 feet (1.5 m) long.

The clam has rows of "eyes" along the edge of its shell. These are so sensitive to light that when a shadow falls across them, such as the shadow of a **predator**, the shell slowly starts to close.

The male cowfish attracts a female by dancing around her. Then, the pair swim up to the surface of the water, where the male hums so loudly to the female that nearby divers can hear him.

The crown-of-thorns starfish, has rows of tube-shaped feet on its underside with strong suckers on the ends. These help the starfish to move around and hold onto the coral.

44

Tiger shark
The tiger shark is a powerful fish that will eat almost anything. Tin cans and license plates have been found inside the stomachs of some tiger sharks.

Anemone fish
The anemone fish has a slimy covering on its body that protects it from the sea anemone's stinging tentacles.

Sea anemone
The sea anemone is an animal that looks like a plant. It anchors itself to the coral and waves its long tentacles through the water.

The tiger shark's pointed teeth have jagged edges that help it to tear its **prey**. Rows of new teeth keep growing inside the shark's mouth to replace older ones that drop out or break.

The sea anemone catches prey, such as shrimps, with its long, stinging tentacles. The tentacles slowly close around the shrimp, which is then passed into the anemone's gaping mouth.

Anemone fish lay their eggs within a sea anemone's tentacles, where the eggs are safe from **predators**. Both parents fan the eggs with water and clean them with their mouths.

Glossary

adapt To change slowly in order to fit in better with your surroundings.

amphibian An animal that lives part of its life in water and part on land. Most lay their eggs and begin their life in water.

Antarctic Circle An imaginary line that circles the southernmost part of the Earth.

Arctic Circle An imaginary line that circles the northernmost part of the Earth.

bill A bird's beak.

bird An animal with feathers, wings, and a bill. Its young hatch from eggs. Birds are warm-blooded, which means the temperature of their bodies is nearly always the same. Most birds can fly.

breed To have babies.

camouflage The markings or colors that can help an animal blend in with its surroundings and hide it from other animals.

climate A pattern of weather in an area that is roughly the same year after year.

continent A huge area of land that is surrounded or nearly surrounded by water. Most of the land that makes up a continent is in one large piece.

coral reef A large ridge of coral that forms in warm seas. Coral is a stony material that is slowly built up from the ocean floor by sea creatures called polyps.

courtship A special performance, such as a dance, done by an animal to attract a partner, or **mate**.

endangered When a type of animal may die out because only a few of its kind are left in the world.

evolved To have developed or changed slowly over millions of years.

extinct No longer living. An animal becomes extinct when no more of its kind are left in the world.

equator An imaginary line that circles the Earth around its middle, halfway between the North and South poles.

fish An animal that lives in water. Most fish have fins and a tail for swimming. Most fish are also cold-blooded, which means the temperature of their bodies stays the same as the water around them.

fresh water Water that is not salty.

hibernate To become sleepy or inactive in winter. Hibernating helps animals to survive cold winters.

insect A small animal with six legs and a hard case, called an exoskeleton, on the outside of its body. Insects have wings and most can fly.

mammal An animal that is warm-blooded, which means the temperature of its body is nearly always the same, and that feeds its young on the mother's milk.

mate A partner. To mate means to form a pair in order to have babies.

mating season A time of year when animals pair together in order to have babies.

migrate To make a regular journey from one place to another.

nectar A sugary substance that is produced by flowers. Many **insects** and **birds** feed on nectar.

nocturnal Active at night. Nocturnal animals sleep during the day and are active at night.

polluted Air, water, or land that is dirty because harmful substances have been put into it.

predator An animal that hunts and eats other living animals.

prey Animals that are hunted and eaten by other animals.

reptile An animal with a dry, scaly body. Its young usually hatch from eggs. Reptiles are cold-blooded, which means the temperature of their bodies is the same as the air around them.

salt water Water that is salty.

scent A smell.

scrubland Land that is dry and covered with small trees and shrubs.

sense Animals use different senses, including seeing, hearing, feeling, tasting, and smelling to tell them about the world around them.

tundra A cold area of land where there are no trees and the soil is often frozen.

wildlife Animal life.

Index

Aardvark 33
adapted 10, 16, 23, 28
Africa 6–7, 36
　Northern 6–7, 30–31
　Southern 6–7, 32–33
alligator 14, 15
　Chinese 39
Alps *see* mountains
Amazon *see* forests
America: Central 6, 16–17
　United States 6, 12–13
amphibians 24, 39
anemone fish 45
anhinga 14
anole lizard 16, 17
Antarctica 6–7, 9, 20
Antarctic Circle 5, 6–7, 9
anteater, giant 18, 19
antelopes 29, 31, 38, 39
ants 17, 18, 19, 43
　army 17
　leaf-cutter 18, 19
Arctic 6–7, 8
Arctic Circle 5, 6–7, 8, 10–11,
　22–23, 26–27
armadillo, nine-banded 19
Asia: Eastern 7, 38–39
　Southeast 7, 40–41
　Southern 7, 36–37
　Southwest 7, 28–29
ass, Asian wild 36, 38
atlas moth 37
Australia 7, 42–43
avocet 24
aye-aye 35

Badger 22, 23, 36
bats 16, 40
　Kitti's hog-nosed 40
　vampire 17
bear: brown 27
　grizzly 10, 13
　polar 8, 11
beaver 11
bee-eater 24, 25
bees 16, 25, 36
bird of paradise 43
birds 9, 10, 11, 13, 14, 16, 17,
　18, 20, 22, 24, 27, 28, 29,
　31, 32–33, 37, 38, 39, 43
bison 12, 13
boar, wild 22, 23, 27
bobcat 10–11
booby, blue-footed 21
breeding 9, 24, 27
buffalo, water 37

Camel: Bactrian 38, 39
　dromedary 28, 29, 31, 39
camouflage 11, 14, 34, 36, 41
Canada 6, 10–11

caracal 29
Caribbean 6, 16–17
cattle 38
chameleon, common 35
chamois 25
cheetah 31
chimpanzee 30, 32–33
chipmunk 12–13
cicada 25
clam, giant 44
climate 12, 14, 16
cobra, king 36, 37
continent 9, 18
coral reefs 43, 44–45
courtship 15, 21, 34, 38
cowfish 44
coyote 13
crab: robber 37, 40–41
　sally-lightfoot 20
crane, Japanese 38, 39
crocodile 31, 38
　estuarine 40
　Nile 31
crown-of-thorns starfish 44

Deciduous forests 5
deer 10, 19, 27, 36, 40
　red 22
deserts 5, 12, 16, 18, 28, 30,
　32, 36, 38
　Atacama 19
　Barren 29
　Gobi 38
　Great Basin 13
　Great Sandy 29
　Great Victoria 42
　Kalahari 33
　Sahara 30–31
　Takla Makan 38
　Thar 36
dinosaurs 42
dolphin: Chinese
　bottle-nosed 25
　river 38, 39
dugong 41
dung beetle 29, 31

Eagle: bald 12
　harpy 18, 19
echidna 42, 43
elephant: African 31, 33
　Asian 36, 37
elk *see* moose
emu 42
equator 5, 6–7, 18–19, 20,
　33, 40–41
ermine 8, 11, 22
Europe: Northern 6–7, 22–23
　Southern 6–7, 24–25
Everglades *see* Florida
evolved 20, 42

Fish 9, 10, 12, 14, 15, 17,
　19, 20, 23, 24, 27, 36, 38,
　39, 40, 44, 45
flamingo 25, 32, 33
Florida Everglades 6, 13,
　14–15
flower mantis 40, 41
forests: deciduous 5
　Amazon 18–19
　evergreen 5, 10, 22
　rain forests 5, 16–17, 18–19,
　32, 34, 36, 40–41
　taiga 26–27
fossa 35
fox: arctic 8
　fennec 28–29
　red 22, 23
frigate bird, magnificent 21
frilled lizard 42
frog: arrow-poison 18, 19
　edible 26–27
　tree 14
funnel-web spider 42

Galapagos Islands 6, 18,
　20–21
gazelle, dorcas 29
gecko: flying 40–41
　leaf-tailed 34
genet, common 25
gharial 36, 37
giraffe 33
gnu 33
golden lion tamarin 19
goliath beetle 32, 33
gorilla 32, 33
grasslands 5, 12, 18, 26, 30,
　36, 38, 39
　pampas 18
　plains 36
　savannah 32–33
Great Barrier Reef 7, 43,
　44–45
Great Rift Valley 32–33

Habitat 5, 38
hamster 26, 27
hare, arctic 8
hedgehog 22
hibernate 26
Himalaya *see* mountains
hippopotamus 33
hognose snake 16–17
honey creeper, Hawaiian 13
horse 38, 39
howler monkey 18
hummingbird, Cuban bee
　16, 17
hyena, spotted 30

Ibis, scarlet 17
ice fish 9
iguana, marine 20
Indian Ocean 7, 40
insects 17, 27, 28, 30, 31,
　32, 34, 35, 41

Jaguar 19
jay, blue 13
jerboa, desert 28, 29
Jesus Christ lizard 16, 17

Kangaroo: red 42, 43
　tree 41
kingfisher 22
kinkajou 16, 17
kiwi 43
koala 42, 43
Komodo dragon 40, 41
krill 9

Lakes 5, 10, 32
　Baikal 27
　Great Bear 10
　Great Lakes 11
　Great Slave 11
　Nyasa 33
　Volta 30
lammergeier 25
lemming 8, 26
lemur 34, 35
　ring-tailed 34
leopard 9, 29
　snow 37
lion 32, 33
lizards 12, 16, 17, 20, 40
　anole lizard 16
　frilled lizard 42
　monitor lizard 28–29
llama 18–19
lynx, Spanish 24, 25

Macaque, Japanese 39
macaw, scarlet 16, 17
Madagascar 7, 33, 34–35
mammals 15, 17, 19, 22, 24, 30, 40–41, 43
manatee 15
manta ray 41
marmot 24–25
mating season 21, 29, 37
meerkat 32, 33
Mexico 6, 16
migration 10, 26
mink 10
mockingbird 13
monarch butterfly 11, 16
mongoose 36
monitor lizard 29
monkeys 18, 19, 28, 29, 40
moose 10, 11, 27
mosquito 27
mountains 5, 10, 18, 24, 26, 28, 32, 36, 39
  Ahaggar 30
  Alps 25
  Appenines 25
  Andes 19
  Atlas 30
  Balkan 25
  Drakensberg 33
  Elburz 29
  Great Dividing Range 43
  Himalaya 36–37, 38
  Pyrenees 24
  Rocky 10, 12, 13
  Sierra Madre 16
  Ural 26
  Yablonovyy 27
  Zagros 29
mouse, Arabian spiny 29
mudskipper 40, 41
musk ox 8

Narwhal 8
nectar 13, 16
New Zealand 7, 42–43
nocturnal 25, 30
numbat 42–43

Ocelot 17
octopus, common 24, 25
orangutan 41
oryx, Arabian 29
osprey 22
ostrich 33
otter 22, 23
owl: fish 39
  snowy 8, 10
oxpecker 31

Pacific Islands 7, 42–43
Pacific Ocean 6–7, 41
pampas see grasslands
panda: giant 38, 39
  red 38–39
pangolin 30
peacock, blue 37
pelican 25, 26, 27
penguin: emperor 9
  Galapagos 20
pheasant, golden 38–39
pigs 19, 29, 36, 40
piranha 19
plains see grasslands
Poles 5, 8, 9
  North Pole 8
  South Pole 9
polluted 38
prairie dog 12, 13
praying mantis 28
predators 15, 32, 35, 45
prey 11, 14, 19, 24, 28, 29, 31, 32, 35, 36, 37, 39, 45
proboscis monkey 40, 41
pronghorn 12
Przewalski's horse 38, 39
ptarmigan 8, 10, 11
puff adder 32–33
puffin 22, 23
Pyrenees see mountains

Quelea, red-billed 30, 31
quetzal, resplendent 16, 17

Raccoon 10, 13, 16, 39
rain forests see forests
ratel 36
rattlesnake 13
reindeer 8, 22, 23, 26, 27
reptiles 13, 20, 22, 24, 34, 36, 42, 43
rhinoceros: Indian 36, 37
  white 30, 31, 33
rivers 5, 23, 36, 38
  Amazon 19
  Amu Darya 26
  Amur 27
  Brahmaputra 37
  Colorado 13
  Danube 22, 25
  Darling 43
  Don 26
  Elbe 22
  Euphrates 29
  Ganges 37
  Helmand 36
  Indus 36
  Irtysh 26
  Lena 27
  Loire 22
  Mackenzie 10
  Mekong 40
  Mississippi 13
  Missouri 13
  Murray 43
  Narmada 37
  Nelson 11
  Nile 31
  Ob 26
  Ohio 13
  Orange 33
  Orinoco 18
  Paranã 19
  Rhone 25
  Rio Grande 13
  São Francisco 19
  Seine 22, 25
  St. Lawrence 11
  Tagus 24
  Tigris 29
  Volga 26
  Yangtze 39
  Yellow 39
  Yenisey 27
  Yukon 10
  Zaire 33
  Zambezi 33
roadrunner 13
Rocky Mountains see mountains
Russia 26–27

Sahara Desert see desert
saiga 38–39
salamander: fire 24, 25
  giant 39
salmon 12
savannah see grasslands
scent 27, 34
scorpions 30, 32
scrubland 24
sea anemone 44, 45
sea birds 22, 23
seal 9
  Baikal 26, 27
  elephant 9
  fur 19
  harp 11
  leopard 9
  monk 24–25
  ringed 8
secretary bird 30, 31
shark 44
  tiger 45
sheep, barbary 30
shrew, tree 36, 37
shrimps 45
sifaka 34
skua 9
skunk 11, 13
sloth 18, 19
snakes 12, 13, 17, 28, 32, 36
South America 6, 18–19, 20
spiders 16, 17, 30, 32, 42
spoonbill, roseate 15
squid 9
squirrel 12, 24, 39
  red 22
stag beetle 22, 23
starfish 44
sturgeon 26
swordfish 17

Taiga see forests
taipan 42
tapir, Malayan 40, 41
tarantula, red-kneed 16, 17
Tasmanian devil 43
termites 18
tern, arctic 8, 9
terrapin, diamondback 14
territory 27
tiger 36, 37
  Siberian 27
  Sumatran 41
tortoise 24, 25
  giant 21
toucan 18, 19
tsetse fly 30, 31
tuatara 42, 43
tundra 8, 26
turtle, snapping 13

United States 6, 12–13

Viper: northern 22
  sand 28, 29
vole 39

Walrus 8
warbler, East Siberian willow 26, 27, 31
waxwing 26, 27
weaverbird 32, 33
whales 9
  beluga 8
  blue 9
  killer 9
wildebeest see gnu
wildlife 42, 44
wolf 8, 10, 13, 23, 25, 26, 27
wolverine 10, 22, 23
wombat 43
woodlands 22
woodpecker, Gila 16

Yak 38